Imagery In You

Mining For Treasure In Your Inner World

Jenny Garrison RN

Outskirts Press, Inc.
Denver, Colorado

Imagery In You
Mining For Treasure In Your Inner World
All Rights Reserved
Copyright © 2006 Jenny Garrison
Cover Image © 2006 JupiterImages Corporation
All Rights Reserved. Used With Permission.

Outskirts Press
http://www.outskirtspress.com

ISBN-10: 1-59800-495-6
ISBN-13: 978-1-59800-495-3

Outskirts Press and the "OP" logo are trademarks belonging to
Outskirts Press, Inc.

Printed in the United States of America

Dedication

This book is about the practice of entering the depths of our beings to bring forth treasures of wisdom and understanding. I dedicate this book to the miners; those men, women and children who, throughout the ages, have gone into the earth itself to bring forth the treasures that adorn us, keep us warm, and delight us.

This dedication also extends to Eligio Stephen Gallegos, my first teacher of imagery. I dedicate this book to him and to all the animals who come as our teachers.

Prologue

This book is about using imagery as a language of the sacred human interior. In an age of unparalleled outward growth of and by the human species, balance is vital and necessary as a stabilizing force. If outer expansion is not balanced by inner expansion, discontent and illness result. Inner expansion connects us as human beings with all creation, with the Earth and her seas, with the stars and the universe, and with our Creator. When enough human beings realize their brotherhood and sisterhood with all that is, the scales will tip toward balance. Eyes will be opened in a new way. Ears will hear in a new way. Earth will be loved in a new way and by the multitudes.

The inner journey is not a selfish one. It is a journey of great unselfishness. As the inner world is explored by mankind, we see in each individual heart the wisdom of infinity, the teaching that lies hidden in all of creation and in every entity and creature. Our heart then returns to its necessary place within the heart of creation. We return to our true self, reclaiming the beauty of our being and its relation to all things. Balance is restored, not only within our physical and emotional bodies but with Earth and all beings as well.

Balance is a lofty aim, but restoration of balance is now the work of us all. Deep imagery work is liberating and joyful. As we use imagery to turn our eyes toward the inner treasures of truth, we see the great world from a different perspective. The gems of knowledge within us come to greet us, and through this process all that we are not falls way, showing us our true home in the great mystery of all that is.

Table of Contents

Foreword

Part One
What Deep Imagery Is All About

Part Two
Doing Imagery

Part Three
A Sampler of Deep Imagery Encounters

Part Four
Some Final Considerations

Foreword

A winter moon illuminates the night. With several decisions to make, I find myself unable to sleep. By profession, I am a guide and teacher of deep imagery. I often tell my students that sleeplessness is a beautiful invitation to do some imagery. In this moment, practicing what I preach, I turn inward.

I ask God to be with me as I relax my body and quiet my thinking. I call forth an image from inside.

I become aware of a sea turtle, swimming in the ocean waters. I greet Sea Turtle and acknowledge Turtle's presence. I ask Turtle, "Do you have a message for me?"

Turtle does not respond in words, but takes me to the bottom of the sea. There, I am shown a treasure chest. Turtle opens the chest and brings forth gems. I listen as Turtle tells me about publishing this book and sharing my knowledge of retrieval of treasures from our depths; about sharing the knowledge of deep imagery. I ask whether this is correct, and turtle responds, "Yes."

Turtle then takes me to a small tree-lined beach. As we come ashore, turtle looks at me and says the word "dangerous." I am a bit shocked. I tell turtle that I don't understand. In my mind's eye, I am then shown a little toy I had as a child. The toy was a small round bug with wheels. The wheels could be revved against the floor to propel the bug forward on its own course, regardless of what was in its way or what was around it. Turtle tells me that I am acting dangerously like that bug, that there are strong deep currents that are part of fully living, and that I am not paying enough attention to these deep and joyful currents of life, that my focus has become too driven and relentless.

And I know this to be true.

I take a deep breath and feel the currents of life around me. I feel the currents of joy and laughter, my husband and children asleep in the quiet house, the innocence of our dog dreaming on the rug beside me. I become aware of the missed joy of every moment spent in single pointed focus, and I feel the admonition to let go, to expand, to move out into those deeper currents of life and see what they have to offer and where they lead.

On this night, Turtle also speaks to me about needing food, showing me how eating is a primitive and almost savage act for turtle. I know the message being given to me is not about literal food, but about partaking in the primal parts of life, birth and death, pain and joy, love and sorrow. This message is about letting go of fear and reigniting my engagement in life.

I have a sense of turtle's body lying over me, on top of me, becoming part of me. I thank turtle, and say good-bye. The world seems like a new place. Something has changed inside me, too. I felt lightness, a willingness to expand, and a sense of adventure.

Sleep came to me like a friend that night after doing this imagery. The new awareness was still with me when I woke, and has lived in me since this imagery transpired.

I have learned to enter into deep imagery, and you can learn this too. This book is your guide. All that you need to embark on your own journey is already inside you. This manual is written to awaken the natural human capacity to do imagery. Everyone can use deep imagery to learn more about themselves and their world. Whether you embark on this journey alone, with a trusted friend, or with a trained guide, you will surely be blessed by what your inner world has to show you. Your imagery is waiting for you.

Part One
What Deep Imagery Is All About

Introduction

Deep in your being you hold a vast reservoir of wisdom and knowledge that barely gets tapped as you live your busy life. Your inner world holds the rhythms of your psyche, the seeds of your destiny, and the flavor and fragrance of your unique self as it has been shaped and formed by the love of your Creator and the infinite wonder of creation. In short, your inner being holds your truth. This is the treasure that resides, hidden, within you. With love and coaxing, you can bring this treasure forward into your everyday life through the practice of deep imagery.

As humans, we become aware of our own personal inner world when something stirs us and takes us inside... perhaps a beautiful piece of music or a poem that gives us goose bumps, a work of art, a beautiful prayer, the stillness of deep meditation, or nature. The choice to explore the inner world that we carry within us is ours to make. *We can call upon this world and ask it to reveal itself to us.* The qualities of imagination are nudged and engaged as we coax the inner truths to come forth. We ask the imagination to show us the wisdom of our depths, to reveal our inner worlds to us. This process is deep imagery.

Deep imagery arises from that indefinable region within you known as the innate imagination. This place, this pervasive treasure-hold, neglects no part of you. Your deep imagination has full access to <u>all</u> the territories of your mind, to the wisdom, needs and sensations of your body, and to the Spirit that both resides within you and links you with the great knowing, or God.

Deep imagery gives you access to the grand reference

manual within, where you can refer to your inner world at any time, on any subject. Your inner world wants you to come home to who you truly are. It will give you what you need if you are willing to go there and to listen, not just with your physical ears but also with your inner senses and full respectful and attentive self.

The Cherokee people have a saying, "Listen, or your tongue will make you deaf!" Listening is an art. Listening is the faculty that must be cultivated as you prepare to converse with your inner world. I use the word "listening" to mean the deep opening of your senses, the careful and full attention that you give to what you are seeing, hearing, and sensing from the inner world. Your inner world will reveal itself to you through images, sounds, smells, memories, words, colors, and feelings. You are then called upon to respond to what you have heard, seen, and sensed. In this way, a conversation will begin. You will find that the direction this conversation takes is literally the road home. The wisdom that created you lives within you, waiting to return you to yourself, waiting to return you to wholeness and love with infinite insight and guidance.

The framework of inner world exploration through imagery is known as the inner journey. It is a journey into the deep imagination. To make this journey, you prepare yourself mentally and physically, and you call forth an image from your depths. With all your receptive abilities, you look and listen with your inner senses and begin a conversation with the images that come to you from your unique inner world. This is deep imagery, and this is the practice that this manual teaches.

You will find that the images that come to you know exactly what you need, even if you are not clear about this in your thinking. The images from within will determine the direction and the unfolding of your journey. You do not have to plan this. In fact, planning will interfere. Your inner world will reveal itself to you through figures of all types, from comical and outrageous to holy and wonderful. You will be led through landscapes wrought with infinite design, where awesome beauty and unheralded normalcy are equal players. You will find that you can trust what comes to you; learning how the images that bring forth feelings of fear are there only to take you to a new place of healing, love, and discovery. You will find that the images that come to you pertain completely to who you really are.

This book will tell you how to prepare for the inner journey. All you need is the time, courage, and willingness that you give to this exploration. Time takes on new, expandable qualities in the inner world. During the time that you give to your imagery, you will be shown just what you need to see, guided where you need to be guided, and taught what you most need to learn as this work gently moves you toward your full potential. The deep intelligence within you wants to show you the path of your greatest growth.

Imagine yourself completely receptive, alert, and responsive to any signal that you perceive from your surroundings or those around you. This is an animal-like sensitivity. All of your senses are on the alert, waiting to receive signals from the world around you. This degree of receptivity is the attentiveness that yields amazing results when you practice it around young children, animals, and the natural world. This receptivity becomes a conversation only when you take the message that you have perceived into yourself and then respond to the perceived message with genuine honesty. In this way, you can find yourself in conversation with a tree, a star, or a purple finch. You become part of the sunset sinking into the mountain or of the sea in the morning with the crabs scurrying for cover. You are "in conversation" with the world around you. You are open and receptive.

In the inner world, this receptivity becomes the way you secure the message you have asked to receive. Perhaps you will sense some words and the feelings that accompany them. This work asks you to take that sensing into yourself as a message and really receive it and respond to it. Deep imagery is often a round about way of learning. Your deep self knows your questions; it will get to them eventually. Perhaps other matters exist that in your innermost being are perceived as primary for the care of your soul. Trust your inner world to deliver what you need.

For example, Marielle wants to know why her boyfriend has lost interest in her. Her inner world shows her a tall angel who brings Marielle a message about beauty. The angel shows her how beauty is reflected by the eyes of love and how she must look out upon the world with eyes of love, how she must cultivate this practice and see what happens... and then see how eyes full of love will start to turn back toward her as she herself develops this way of seeing. Marielle leaves her imagery session with a practice that has been prescribed by her own true knowing in the form of a tall angel. She now has a new assignment; to look at the world and at others through the eyes of love. This is a practice that will nourish her soul. Her deep self did not see the boyfriend issue as one of primary importance, but rather as a doorway to an area of deeper growth and deeper learning about love. This is how the process works. The inner world sifts through the chaff and offers the unique kernels of core wisdom.

A deep imagery journey opens and closes with acknowledgment of who or what has come forth for you. The journey time is literally filled with the knowledge of the inner world as it comes to you from your imagery. The knowledge that you glean from your inner journey becomes part of you and part of your life as you re-enter the outer world of everyday awareness. Your inner knowing changes and completes you, bringing you home to who you truly are.

For many of us, our imaginations have not been this awake since we were children. Nor have they been given the credit of consultation in our lives. We must symbolically clear a space to do this exploration. We must start from a fresh place of newness in our minds, asking the inner world to come to us, to reveal our true selves to us through the images, words, and stories that come from own depths. We must sweep away the cobwebs of accumulated mistrust and cynicism that cloud our imaginations, calling forth the wonders of the inner world and unearthing the treasures of truth within us.

Your inner world is always with you. It is always available. You can truly knock at your own door and gather what you know of your truest self. The ability to engage in deep imagery is not limited to a gifted few but offered to each of us through a God-given ability that is individually unique and yet present in everyone. Deep imagery is the language your inner world uses to reveal itself to you. It asks only for the conscious engagement of your imagination and inner listening as you explore your world and your being from an inner perspective.

Chapter One
Working with the Recipe

Recipes are old-fashioned magic. They list ingredients and offer instructions for blending and preparing those ingredients so that something new and delicious can result. The word "recipe" originally referred to medicinal formulas. This limited meaning then expanded into the arts of home, hearth, and food preparation. Recipes, or lists of ingredients and how they are combined, are usually written in simple form so they can be easily followed. Changes are likely to occur in the final result as each person using the recipe adds to or subtracts from it, adding special touches or substituting ingredients. The recipe itself is meant to be a basic instruction, a basic formula. It individualizes with each cook but stands as a useful direction for anyone wishing to follow it toward its final result. I have used this old and familiar model of a recipe to write about doing imagery. The recipe that follows will lead you into relationship with the images and messages that live inside you. In my work with imagery, I have seen a great need for a simple tool that can be used by people to access their inner realms. That need led to this simple recipe which can be memorized or bookmarked for reference. Perhaps this recipe will fill in some ingredients that may be missing in your attempts to journey to the inner world, or perhaps this will be your first real ticket to your inner world and the riches that lie there waiting to be revealed. The recipe is given as a gift, as a simple formula of direction that will help you to unearth the riches of your own truth. This recipe will help you to receive the images and messages that are a part of your inner knowing. You may individualize it in any way that works for you.

Your inner world waits to reveal to you the immensity of your being. Your imagery waits to tell you about yourself and how you relate to the rest of the world. Your inner world is full of treasure, wisdom, and truth. Experiment with this recipe. It will bring you many surprises, the sure knowledge that you are part of something great, and the assurance that you are never alone.

Use the recipe on the following page as you journey inward. It can be placed in front of you or used as a resource or key if you are guiding or being guided by another. You may want to copy it onto a recipe card for easy reference. This recipe is your companion for a fruitful inner journey.

The Recipe

1. Protect the space. Pray.
2. Quiet your mind. Relax your body.
3. Invite an image to come forth.
4. Enter the emerging story, using the five essential ingredients.

The 5 Essential Ingredients

- Greet the image. Thank it for coming.
- Ask the image whether it has a message for you, something to show or tell you.
  > ("Listen" with all of your inner senses for an answer. Respond honestly.)
- Ask the image whether it needs anything.
  > ("Listen" with all of your inner senses for an answer. Respond honestly.)
- Ask whether anything more needs to happen.
  > ("Listen" with all of your inner senses for an answer. Respond honestly.)
- Thank the image for coming.
  > (You may ask the imagery for a parting gift of words, images, or a gesture.) Say "good-bye" in a way that feels right.

5. Readjust to the outer, physical world.
6. Record your journey.
7. Integrate your journey.

Always be real. Always be honest. Allow yourself freedom in your inner world. It is your world. Be respectful. Stay with what is happening. Be sure to include the five essential ingredients.

As with any recipe, ingredients may be added, subtracted, or substituted to alter the recipe according to personal taste.

Part Two

Doing Imagery

Chapter Two

Pray
Protect the Space

The simple act of shifting your awareness toward the presence of God will offer protection and welcome Spirit into your inner journey.

When embarking on an outward journey in the physical world, the common practice of a traveler's prayer invites protection and blessing to accompany you as you enter new and unknown territories. Prayer brings awareness to the presence of Spirit and invites the accompaniment of this presence as you prepare for your inner journey too. Pray in whatever way you as an individual do that. Prayer can take many forms. Let it be natural. Let it flow from whatever you know and whoever you are. For some, the act of honoring the inner silence becomes their prayer. For others, the conscious asking that God be with you as you "look" within constitutes all or part of the prayer. Prayer can ride on the breath as you bring awareness to your breathing.

I sometimes burn white sage in the Native American custom of smudging as preparation for entering the sacred space of the inner world. This is an example of a personal prayer style or ritual. Let your prayer be your own.

Perhaps certain prayer words have held meaning for you. You can softly speak them as you turn inward. Some prayer words that I love come from a story I read as a very young woman (The Scent of Water, by Elizabeth Goudge).

They are simple, strong, and always in my mind. I'll share them with you here:

Lord have mercy.
Thee I adore.
Into thy hands.

However you choose to pray, know that the deliberate turning toward Spirit at the beginning of your travels to the inner world will influence and inform what occurs there. Alignment with Spirit brings protection from the fear of evil. It magnifies your intent to reach toward wholeness and goodness. This alignment with Spirit will amplify the trust you can have in the stories, teachings, and information that come to you from your inner world of imagery.

Just as prayer protects your inner being during imagery, a few preparations in the physical world can enhance your ability to travel inward.

Try to do your imagery in an environment that is free from distraction. This is not always necessary (or possible!) but can be helpful, especially at the beginning. Even though your eyes may be closed, dim light is helpful and will facilitate inner "seeing." A cloth or an eye-bag over your eyes can help to rest your physical vision and draw your attention inward.

Protect the area to the extent that you can practically do this. This protectiveness may take the form of turning off the telephone or closing the door. Minimizing the chance of disturbance will increase your feeling of safety, thus helping you to relax and let go in your imagery. Find a position that is comfortable. If you are at all tired, choose to sit rather than to lie down.

Once you become comfortable engaging your imagery, you will be able to consult your inner world in this way even in the midst of distraction. Remember, though, that the creation of a held space in which to do your imagery honors and supports your inner journey, especially when you are first learning to engage your imagery.

Chapter Three

Quiet Your Mind, Relax Your Body: Sky, Earth, Fire, and Water

T ake in a deep breath and then let it out. Allow your shoulders to relax. Drop your awareness to a place deep in your body, in the region of your gut and belly. Let your knees relax. Feel the place where your feet touch the floor.

On an inner level, a return occurs when you surrender your body instead of holding it tightly. This surrender deepens your connection with your inner rhythms as you reach toward your source, your center. To enter this inner rhythm is to enter the river that carries you to your inner world. It is also, in itself, a place of deep refreshment and rejuvenation.

As you turn within, a helpful practice involves bringing to mind what is above and below; sky and Earth. Your breathing connects you intimately with the sky. Your body and its support connect you deeply with the earth. Making the internal connection with sky and Earth will assist the quieting of your mind and support the deep relaxation in and of your body.

Sky and Earth

When you breathe in, or inhale, you are taking air into your body. Reach now, with your mind, and consider this act of breathing air. What is it that you are taking into your body? In truth, it is the sky.

The sky holds the atmosphere that surrounds our planet. Breathe it in. What you are breathing is the air that has circulated into the place where you are, right now, as you read this. This same air has been breathed by millions of other beings, including animals and all sorts of humans. The air you breathe has been refreshed by plants and trees. Leaves have fallen through it, as has rain and maybe snow. It is the invisible blanket through which you view the night sky. You are utterly dependent upon it. Without it, your body dies within a short period of time.

Every time you breathe in, this sky air enters your body. Every time you breathe out you release the by-product of your in-breath, which is no longer needed. This breathing in and breathing out is the process of respiration. Carbon dioxide, which we breathe out as the by-product of respiration, is then recycled by the green world of plants and trees. Your breath is an intimate part of the larger cycle of life itself.

Breathe in. Pay attention to the act of breathing and the sensation of breath as it moves into you and out of you. The substance of this air you are now breathing finds its way to every cell of your body. Renewal happens with each breath regardless of your awareness that it is occurring. This exchange of air has been happening since the moment of your birth, your first breath. It will happen until that unknown day when you take your last breath. Breathing accompanies you through every moment of your life.

Many methods exist for working with breath, but for quieting the mind and relaxing the body, try simply following your breath. Imagine the fresh sky air going to all parts of you. Follow the exhale too. Breathe out that which will find the plants and trees. Breathe out that which you no longer need, releasing it back into the air. This released air has tenderly traveled into you and out of you. The gift of air sustains your life. Observe it as it moves through you.

Your breathing body is formed of many materials. Your body is your home while you are alive on Earth. In many creation stories the human body is made of Earth.

Reach, now, into the thought of Earth. Imagine it beneath you. Even if you are in an airplane, the earth is still beneath you. If you are on a ship in the middle of the ocean, the earth is the ocean floor beneath you. If you are in a building, you may need to reach through many layers of floors until you connect with the earth, but you will find it there beneath you. Even in a city where a patch of clear ground is rare, the earth is silently supporting the entire structure of the city.

Whenever I am in a big city, I like to reach down with my mind and make connection with the earth below. This reach travels through so many layers: sidewalks, subways, water systems, and underground passages. Ultimately, though, the earth itself is always there, supporting you and all that lies between you and it. The earth supports and sustains you. Without the earth you have nowhere to set your foot, nothing to eat, and no place to live.

As a human, you are intimately tied to Earth. Your body is composed of many of the same elements that compose the earth. The salinity of the fluids of your body is the same as that of Earth's seas. Your form and the form of the earth share similar arrangements. The arteries and veins in your body are like the waterways of the planet. The structure of bronchia and alveoli within the lungs are similar in appearance to upside-down trees with leaves.

When you die, your body will go back to the earth. When your loved ones die, you bury their bodies or scatter their ashes in and on the earth. Earth is home while you are here.

Consider this. Reach for your connection with Earth. Doing this is not difficult because a deep innate association exists between your body and the earth. Feel the place where your body touches the floor and reach with your mind to feel the earth supporting you.

Now, link the two together in your mind... sky and Earth, breath and body. Imagine the round earth surrounded by the sky. Breathe the sky into the earth of your body. Bring your awareness to this. Relax. You are part of everything. You are connected with everything.

This reaching toward Earth and sky will bring you home to your depths as you travel within to the place where they come together. This is a place of deep belonging, a place where imagery can begin.

The more often you make this conscious connection, the easier it becomes. If you are pressed for time, a minute or two is all you need. The uniting of sky, breath, Earth, and body happens easily in our awareness because this unity already exists as part of our physical environment -- patient, constant, and strong-- within and without.

When you willfully make this association, your thinking becomes quiet, and your body deepens its ease. The connection becomes a doorway to the inner world and the world of imagery.

Fire and Water

Our ancestors lived in deep communion with the mysteries and rhythms of nature and honored the natural elements that comprise life. This honoring was a part of nearly all primal cultures. Fire and water were praised along with Earth and sky. As I studied imagery and learned the magic of relaxing into Earth and sky, I often wondered about fire and water.

What I have come to believe is that the fire and water are within us. The presence of fire in the human being is visible in the mysterious unity of heart, mind, and action. The beating of the heart is fired by electrical impulse. Heartbeats mark the rhythms that accompany all of your journeys, inner and outer. Messages travel to and from your brain on the highway of nerves that is your spinal cord. It is here that outside stimuli are changed into the sparks of energy that carry surges of impulse along nerve paths to the brain, where the new communication is perceived and interpreted. And always, behind the scenes, the heart marks time with its steady drum-like rhythm.

Fire is in the spark that ignites the will as we choose to seek the inner images. Fire exists in the alchemy that brings the images forth.

Water is the subconscious, the deep place of all that is submerged. We live on a water planet. Our bodies are comprised chiefly of water. Water denotes our depths, the place where we dive with our awareness as we call forth an image.

I often work with the image of an iceberg when explaining imagery to my students. A tiny portion of the ice is visible above the surface of the water, and beneath this is a great ice mass hidden in the depths. I use this image to visually represent the knowledge that is visible to us in relation to all the knowledge that we truly hold.

Relax with Earth and air; allow your intention to ignite the fire of your seeking as you step into the waters of your depths. Go to the place where your journeys begin.

Chapter Four
Invite an Image to Come Forth

T his moment in inner work is exciting and surprising. Your invitation for an image to come forth arouses the inner world and offers the gift of life to the unknown images inside you.

This invitation is spoken silently. Many types of images can be invited, and the invitation may be very specific or very general. Examples of images that can be requested are reviewed in Part Three of this book. I will speak here of the invitation itself.

The request is made on a silent, inner level, inviting the image to "please come forth." Then, you open your inner senses and wait for a response from the inner world. Perhaps an image will come to you right away. Sometimes people see their imagery almost like figures on a movie screen behind their closed eyes. Images materialize in different ways for everyone. With time and practice, you will become familiar with the way your inner images reveal themselves to you. If an inner sense other than vision is prominent for you, you may "hear" a response to your invitation instead of seeing one, or you may just experience a gut-level knowing. Probably, though, you will be aware of a combination of information. Sometimes the sense of an image will be present, but it will not feel complete or full. That's okay. Just be with what is there as it has come to you. If you are not certain of what you "see," let the image know that. Ask whether it would be willing to become clearer. You may need to begin with a partial image and see what happens.

Trust what comes to you. This is important. The image,

thought, or sense that comes to you may not be what you wanted or expected, but it will be what has answered your invitation. See what it has to convey to you. Great wisdom sometimes comes from a totally unexpected source.

Allow yourself to let go and be surprised by what comes. Surrender is part of this waiting and is part of the alchemy that allows the image to come forth.

Doubt can be a saboteur at this stage. Distrusting the validity of the image you perceive, thinking "I am making this up," or "I am seeing this because I just saw a picture of one of those" are all common aspects of doubt. Don't let these doubting thoughts undermine your imagery. Your sub-conscious has infinite images from which it will choose. It will bring forth an image that will be a perfect match for your inquiry or request. Perhaps the match will be made by an image of something you have seen very recently. This image comes because it is readily available. If the image didn't match your request, it would not be there. Perhaps your subconscious will dig deep into your past for an image, or into the deep collective pool of archetypal images. You don't need to worry about how or why a certain image comes to you. The mechanism is automatic and innate in your being. In fact, this retrieval of images by the inner world is not something you can control anyway. So just trust what comes and work with it. Your thinking mind can examine your imagery when you are done, but at this stage try to remain open and trusting.

Even an image that at first seems fearful often transforms and offers great teachings over time. Be patient and accepting of the images that come to you.

Don't be surprised if images similar in form or energy to the ones you have seen in your inner journey begin to be apparent in the world around you. Often the messages of imagery are affirmed by something you see or hear in the physical world, something you read, an experience you have, or a coincidence that occurs in your life. As we choose to seek and find the guidance that leads to our wholeness, life offers its wisdom from both worlds, inner and outer.

Doubting voices that would keep you from the riches of your inner world exist. These voices will decrease as you become more trusting and practiced. Know that many voices of doubt and rejection are common and stay with the truth of your imagery. At first, you may need to pretend that you trust. As you practice imagery and witness the understanding and assistance that it offers for living your life, the presence of trust in your inner wisdom will grow and bloom within you.

Chapter Five

Enter the Emerging Story

When you turn your attention inward and call forth an image, you have engaged your inner world. It now becomes essential to <u>stay with</u> what is happening. When I learned this aspect of imagery, my teacher taught me that the movement of staying connected with one's imagery was similar to that of stitching cloth with a needle and thread. The needle weaves in and out of the cloth while always returning to it, always connecting the thread (your questions, thoughts, and feelings) with the cloth (the image that has come to you). You receive the image, you take it in, and then you return to the image with a question, acknowledgment, or other response. You respond to what you have heard or been shown.

And so the "conversation" becomes a flowing thing, and it flows between you and the image that has come to you.

Getting to this level of inner conversation requires some focus, but your thinking mind can help you get there. It can stand "sentry," seeing that you stay connected with your imagery. In essence, you give it a job.

This step is not necessary if you are working with a guide, someone whose job it is to keep you connected with your imagery. If you are doing your imagery independently, you must *remember* to stay connected with this back-and-forth flow of conversation by using the five essential ingredients.

1. Greet the image. Thank it for coming.
2. Ask the image whether it has a message for you, something to show or tell you. "Listen" with all of your inner senses for an answer. Respond honestly.
3. Ask the image whether it needs anything. "Listen" with all of your inner senses for an answer. Respond honestly.
4. Ask whether anything more needs to happen. "Listen" with all of your inner senses for an answer. Respond honestly.
5. Thank the image for coming. (You may ask the imagery for a parting gift of words, images or a gesture.) Say "good-bye" in a way that feels right.

You are immersed in the imagery, and on another level you are remembering to stay connected with it and to include the five essential ingredients.

Part of you is witnessing the imagery that is occurring. If you find yourself drifting, return to your imagery with self-compassion. This drifting is very common and very human. By witnessing what is occurring within you and returning to it, you develop skill for staying present and connected with your imagery.

Using the Five Essential Ingredients

1. Greet the image. Thank it for coming.

When you have the sense of the image you have called forth, acknowledge it with a greeting. Let the greeting be natural. It may be a simple "hello." It may be a bow or a nod of the head. Greet the image in a way that feels right for you.

You will be helped here by remembering and following

simple rules of courtesy. This image is an invited guest. Greet it and thank it for coming. This thanking becomes an acknowledgment that the inner world is revealing itself to you at your request.

Even after hundreds of inner journeys, this step remains essential. It is like counting your blessings. When they are acknowledged, they increase.

When your inner world is respectfully acknowledged, it becomes easier to access and more fully available to you. It "increases."

2. <u>Ask the image whether it has a message for you, something to show or tell you.</u>

The particular image that comes to you has come for a reason. It will let you know why it has come. This may happen in a clear, succinct way, but more likely it will "tell" you in stories and metaphor, showing you things, taking you places, and teaching you in its own way through anecdotes, images, feelings, memories, and inner travels.

Ask these questions: "Do you have a message for me?" "Do you have something to show or tell me?" Then open all your inner senses as you wait for a response. "Listen" to what you hear with your inner hearing. Allow yourself to become very receptive. Respond honestly to that which you are being told or shown. If you have feelings, questions, or a need for clarification, let the image know this. Ask it. This keeps the two of you connected. This step in the five essential ingredients may take just a moment, or a whole scenario might unfold. Remain attentive and let the message come to you in its own way.

3. <u>Ask the image whether it needs anything.</u>

A very old custom reminds us to offer food, drink, and rest to a guest. This custom embodies a demonstration of hospitality. It allows a guest to feel welcomed and received with attentiveness. This sets the tone in which this question enters your imagery.

Ask the question "Is there anything you need?" Once again, "listen." Be receptive and alert. Open your inner senses and "hear" the answer.

Ask yourself whether you are willing to give the image what it has asked for. Be honest. If you are able and willing, go ahead and give the image what it needs. If you are not able or willing, tell the image. Tell it why. Be true to who you are, for the image is part of you, too. Dishonesty yields no benefit in your inner world. Be as honest as you can be. This practice of self honesty becomes easier as you work with it. You will notice that this in itself will help you to grow in ways of understanding.

You have resources in the inner world that are not available to you in the physical world, so be creative. If the image asks for food, know that you have within you the imaginative power to produce the exact food that has asked for! Don't hesitate to honor a request from the inner world if doing so feels right.

4. <u>Ask whether anything more needs to happen.</u>

This question enlarges the inner response. It allows the inner world to show you what it feels you need to know. Perhaps some aspect of this teaching will move you toward wholeness. Subject matter of which you are consciously unaware may come to light. Part of the beauty of "looking" inside is this offering by the inner world of information that you don't even know you need! Many times that which is revealed is exactly what you need to know, even though you are unaware that this is what you required.

A physician friend of mine who uses imagery in his work says he finds working with imagery to be very <u>efficient.</u> Something that may take a long time to uncover using other means comes forward readily from the subconscious when using imagery.

So ask the image that has come to you whether anything more needs to happen. This request "passes the ball" back to the inner world, which then comes forward with a response of its own.

If the response or sense that you receive is that nothing more needs to happen, accept that response as invitation for closure. The imagery then moves to completion with the fifth essential ingredient.

5. <u>Thank the imagery. Say "good-bye" in a way that feels right to you.</u>

A gesture of closure is important. You are leaving the inner world and are nearly ready to return to the outer, physical world. At this point of closure, you may ask your inner world for words, a gesture, or an image that you can carry out into your physical world. These words, gestures, or images act as a reminder to your everyday awareness. They help you to hold and recall the messages and energy of the inner imagery. Metaphorically, this parting gift is akin to returning from a trip with a photograph or souvenir that reminds you of where you have been. This reminder from your inner world helps you to recall the energy of your imagery and the learning that accompanies it.

Say good-bye to the images that have come to you, and thank them. Sometimes, the image or images will want to say good-bye to you in a certain way. Sometimes you will want to say good-bye to them in a certain way. The possibilities are endless. Energetic differences (handshake/kiss, formal bow/hug, spoken good-bye/gesture of good-bye) will depend upon the type of imagery that has occurred for you and the relationship that has developed naturally between you and the images you have met. Allow room for this natural parting.

Many times, more than one image will come forth in the

course of your inner traveling. Thank them all, giving acknowledgment to each of them as part of closure.

As crossing to the inner world becomes more frequent and more comfortable, the impressions you receive there will weave themselves into a story or "journey." The natural movement of your inner world is toward wholeness, toward your center, and toward reconnection with your sacred self. Allowing the inner world to reveal itself brings forth teachings, information, and sometimes suggestions and advice within the unfolding story.

Your ability to allow this unfolding requires trust and letting go. You have the faculties you need to do this. You were born with them. They are gifts. Just trust and follow what is happening. When questions arise, stay connected with the imagery by posing your questions to the image. When feelings arise, honor them by voicing them to the image. Honor emotions, too. Laughter and tears are part of you. Let your emotions be part of your inner work, staying connected with the imagery instead of breaking away from it. When you are unsure of what you are experiencing, ask the image for more clarity. If you don't understand something that is happening, tell the image about that lack of understanding. If you find yourself doubting your imagery, be honest, express your doubts. Let the image or images know what you are really feeling.

Stay with what is happening. Just as in outer stories, and in life, new characters may enter the scene. The theme may change, only to circle back later to the original inquiry. Feeling tone may change. Stay with it. Notice. Open yourself to this story which belongs to you and which connects your true self with the rest of the universe. Be attentive. Be truthful.

What have you got to lose? No one else needs to see or know what you are doing. You have total freedom to be very honest with the imagery of your inner world. A child-like playfulness and innocence, along with trust and surrender, will bring your inner world to new life and bring you closer to the wonder of who you are. Often, these qualities of playfulness, innocence, trust, and surrender have been dulled by the requirements of adult life, but they are there, inside, and will respond to you. So be easy on yourself. Be persistent. Sometimes, waking something that has been asleep takes a long time.

Let your guidelines be the simple rules of hospitality, respect, and the five essential ingredients. Be attentive. Stay honest. Stay in connection with what comes forward by dialoguing with it. Participate in the conversation.

If the story line changes, trust this new direction. You can always come back to your original inquiry before leaving your inner world. The direction that surprises you may be taking you where you most need to go. Being unwilling to do what the journey asks is okay too. Just be honest.

Work with whatever comes. Eventually, or maybe right away, journeys will develop around the images. The word journey describes the venture of travel from one place to another, and all that it entails. Your images will weave themselves into conversations and journeys. With your assistance, your journeys will influence and change your life with their wisdom, guidance, and silent offer of true sustenance.

Chapter Six
Readjusting To the Outer World

Give yourself some time and space for readjustment as you leave the inner world of imagery and enter the outer world of physical awareness. This brief period of transition calls for some kindness to yourself, so don't rush.

As you open your eyes, your surroundings may seem bright and your consciousness slightly altered. This response is natural. The shift between the worlds will become less obvious as your travels to the inner world become more frequent and as you become more accustomed to the passage between the inner and outer worlds.

Awareness of breathing and of the senses is a trustworthy and gentle way to make the transition. Just as you used breathing and attunement to the inner senses to help you enter the inner world, you can use the same faculties to exit these realms, only this time the emphasis of awareness is with the senses and sensations of the physical world to which you are returning.

With your eyes still closed, begin to shift your sensory awareness to the physical world. Become aware of any sounds. Feel the touch of your clothes against your skin. Recall Earth, sky, body, and breath now, and be aware of the ground that supports your body. Be aware of Earth beneath you. Feel the support of the chair or floor as it meets your body. Breathe. Become conscious of air moving through your body. Don't try to change your breathing, just follow it. Feel it moving from the outside in and the inside out.... the same directions you have just traveled! Taking this time as you depart from your inner world will help you to feel alert and grounded as you make the transition back into the physical world.

Open your eyes. Notice how the world looks new and fresh as you make passage from the inner world to the outer.

Often a stillness of the body occurs during imagery, so reintroduce movement in a gentle way as you take a nice stretch that feels good to your body.

You have accomplished the crossing. Just as when you physically travel to a new place and find yourself feeling different and refreshed when you return, you are now holding the subtle energies of the inner places wherein you have traveled, the teachings you have received, and the helpers with whom you have met and communicated. You now carry these reclaimed energies with you into your life.

Chapter Seven
Record Your Journey

Take the time to record the images, stories, and impressions you have received during your inner journey. This written record is important! I have learned this truth through my own work with imagery and through guiding others into their imagery. Without this initial recording, details of the journey fade. They become less available to you, and more elusive.

When you record your journey, it is there in front of you, mined from your inner depths and real in your hands. Now you can work with it. Your thinking mind can see how it fits with your life. You can share it with a friend or counselor. You can ponder it quietly and privately as you examine the words you have written and the messages you have received. What was once deep in your subconscious has taken form once again and is present for you now in what you have recorded as the written word.

The stories, teachings, and impressions that come from the depths of your being are valuable, even priceless. The difference between reading what someone else has to say about what you may need vs. what your own deep self has to say about what you may need is substantial. The messages of your imagery disclose the counsel of your own depths. These words are often interlaced with humor and metaphor. They are totally unique to you. Putting them on paper preserves them for your use now and later.

Often, a written journey becomes even more significant as time passes. The teachings seem to ripen as they are brought together with your living. You may look back and discover ways in which the imagery's teachings have influenced and helped you. You may become aware of physical events for which the imagery helped you to prepare. Like wine, the teachings and stories of your imagery become even finer and more precious as they age, seasoning and accompanying your life as their meaning and relevance come to greater and greater light.

Chapter Eight
Integrate Your Journey

The material that comes to you from your inner world is full of meaning. Your inner work will be stronger if you give it a place in your life. The blending of your inner world of imagery with the details and rhythms of your outer life is called integration. The two worlds come together, each influencing the other. Acknowledgement of some kind is required from you for integration to take place. This acknowledgement usually involves some action on your part. Your action may be as simple as contemplation of the imagery, or it may be as bold and creative as a major change of course. The forms that integrative actions take are very individual.

If your recorded journey is stuffed away in a drawer or notebook and given none of your attention, it remains lifeless and non-integrated. How can you give your journey a place of honor in your physical world? I will offer some examples, but perhaps you will think of ways that are unique to you and your own style of living.

I have learned some valuable things about integration through my study of the practice of yoga. The final posture in a hatha yoga practice is called Shavasan, or corpse pose. This is a resting pose during which you lie on your back with your body comfortably supported. Then you let go. You let go of any holding and tension in your body. You let go of thoughts that are chasing you. You let go of any feelings of self-consciousness. You let go of as much as you can. The entire yoga practice comes together during this final posture.

Integration happens through surrender, through letting go and allowing the integration to take place. You do not make it happen, but you set yourself up for it by allowing time for that posture at the end of your practice, by supporting your body, and by being there with your intention to release. This type of organic integration is not confined to a yoga practice. The pattern of conscious action followed by letting go is a natural way to integrate the things that happen in your life. It is also a beautiful and effective way to integrate your imagery journeys.

Set yourself up for surrender to integration. Do the actions first. Put reminders of your inner images and journeys into your outer world. Don't neglect the information that has been given to you. Review it. If you are willing, do what has been asked. Through surrender the inner moves to the outer. The integration will happen. You don't have to force it.

Sometimes you will feel like you just don't "get" or understand the imagery that has come to you. This feeling is okay. Just stay close to the imagery by any of the following suggested approaches. Let the imagery work on and through you. You don't need to "get it" for it to help you. Just stay aware of the imagery and do what it suggests. The imagery's meaning may become more apparent with time. It came from the deep and wise part of you and will work with you in a subtle way as you go about your life. Just remember it often and honor it through acknowledgement and action. Get to know it.

Here are some ideas for actions that will promote integration of your imagery:

-Draw, paint, or craft an image or idea from your journey. Let the art be present in your home or workplace, in a spot you choose carefully. The drawing, painting, or crafted image will embody the energies of your inner journey. Those energies will then have a place in your outer world, where they can blend subtly with the physical world.

Every time you see the art or object, a bit of integration will take place on some level.

-Buy yourself a gift that symbolizes something from the journey. A piece of clothing or jewelry that is representative of something you have been shown by your inner imagery will remind you of your imagery and what it has shown you. You literally wear it. The article, then, will gently connect you with your inner depths, and will be seen by yourself and others as a part of you.

-Transcribe your recorded journey by typing it. The printed word embodies something that suggests knowledge and learning. Seeing your work in this form validates your imagery. Also, the act of typing the written journey takes you through it once again. Almost always, new insights arise. When you type and save your journey, it is organized and available to you physically for reference.

-Journaling can help you to become aware of certain parts of your imagery that your mind didn't hold or recognize at first. As you journal or write out free form thoughts about your imagery, you become aware of relationships between your life and the messages of the imagery. Journaling is a powerful tool for many people. Feelings and perceptions that did not quite come to light during the imagery can often be discovered as you let the pen move on the paper, using journaling as an avenue for deepening expression and understanding.

-Honor any commitments you have made with your inner world. This gesture is respectful and will keep you in good relationship with your imagery. Remember the metaphor of the invited guest? Suppose the guest asked something of you and you said "yes." Then suppose you forgot all about it. Suppose this insult (even if unintentional) happened several times. The energy of the relationship would probably begin to wane. You want to keep your inner world in strong and good standing, where you can interact with it readily. Show it respect. Honor commitments by following through with them. More learning frequently occurs as you follow suggestions and do the work that has been prescribed within your imagery.

-Read your journey or review it in your mind. Notice the images that stand out for you. Think about these images, re-visit them, and hold them in your awareness. The times before and just after sleep are ripe portals for integration. If you have trouble sleeping, recall or revisit your imagery. Sometimes when I find myself unable to sleep, I wonder whether sleep is elusive because I need this conscious time with the inner world. Then I do some imagery. Try it!

-Create an affirmation that reflects the attributes your journey has shown you. Let the affirmation remind you of your inner journey and its energy. An affirmation is a statement that reaches into the creation of the future by using present tense words that go beyond your present reality. Affirmations help you to change the way you think. Let's say your journey revolved around the need for increased physical strength. Your affirmation might be, "My body is strong and powerful." Choose words from your journey as you create a positive statement that you can repeat to yourself many times during the day. Perhaps a specific image from the journey can accompany the words in your affirmation. You can write your affirmations on cards to remind yourself of them. Put the written affirmations in key places where they will elicit your attention (cupboards, mirrors, in your wallet). Say them often, silently or out loud. They are a powerful tool of integration, and any action that embodies an affirmation builds support for integration of the imagery's message.

-Use an image from your inner world as a mantra. A mantra is typically a holy sound or a word that is repeated over and over again. Repetition allows the mantra to influence you on many levels. It can be chanted or spoken silently or out loud. Choose an image or group of words from your inner work that stands out as particularly powerful or that has great meaning for you. At intervals during your day, bring the image or group of words to mind and hold them in your awareness. If it is words, you can repeat them. If it is an image, you can etch it in your mind, coming back to it again and again. Do this when you are stopped in traffic, when you are falling asleep or waking up, or when you are in solitude.

-Perhaps a certain posture comes to you in your imagery. Assuming this posture with your physical body is a wonderful way to bring the imagery home. A helpful and appropriate request during the imagery asks that a posture or a gesture be shown to you that will remind you of your imagery and help you to remember it in your body. I will give an example. I was once working with someone whose inner journey was all about opening her awareness to the gifts that life had given her, rather than what she lacked. During her journey she was shown a hand gesture where her open palms were extended together at heart level in front of her, her hands slightly cupped. She used this gesture to help integrate her journey, spending a quiet minute in this posture before she wrote in her daily gratitude journal. (The journal was her own idea of a way she could work with the teachings she had received from her imagery on a deep inner level.)

*

Be creative. There are many ways to honor and integrate your journey. I have offered a few ideas.

Anything that you introduce into the physical world that reminds you of the inner journey will assist you in clearing the pathway that exists between your inner and outer selves. With integration, understanding of the freedom and beauty of your depths will become a part of your everyday life, and that knowledge will become a constant companion.

Chapter Nine

Troubleshooting: Working With Frequently Encountered Challenges During Imagery

You cannot do imagery "wrong." Stumbling blocks may arise, as they do in any new endeavor, but most of the time these hurdles are just parts of learning to trust and understand the unique language of your inner world. Deep imagery comes from the place within where you are innocent and clean. It comes from the place of worthiness within you. You have a heartfelt knowing in you that wants only to care for you and bring you to your full growth. When working with imagery, you will find that the journeys that come to you are relevant. The inner world always offers exactly what you need. If your journey contains frightening images, those images are there to teach you and to help you grow, not to hurt you. The potential for learning, moving forward, and understanding is unlimited in your inner world. Take small steps forward and stay aware of any feelings of reluctance, fear, mistrust, rejection, or loss of focus. These stumbling blocks are common challenges to deep imagery and you can overcome them.

Reluctance

One of the greatest obstacles that you may encounter as you enter into deep imagery is the sense of reluctance that arises from anticipation of the unknown. As humans, we tend to stay in a place of familiarity and comfort, even if that place no longer serves our growth and greatest good. Bravery is required to overcome the reluctance to step into new territories, be they physical, emotional, or even spiritual. New territories are not part of our known zones of comfort, and as humans, we tend to shy away from them because of lack of skill and experience in a new situation. Have patience. Skill with imagery develops as you become a seasoned journeyer, and reluctance to engage in imagery diminishes. The inner world is no longer foreign territory when you have visited there many times.

Your willingness to visit your inner world will grow as you see for yourself that your own imagery offers you only what you are able to work with and use for growth and healing. The new territories you are shown in your imagery may be previously unknown to you, but they are full of potential for growth and healing. Comfort in new territories is built with time and experience. You cannot know or foresee what might arise from the inner depths. For many people this gives rise to a certain anxiety, so knowing that your imagery comes forth from you to serve your growth is a reassuring foundational point.

The images from your inner world will present themselves in relation to where you are and who you are. What comes forward will not be too much for you. The imagery that comes to you will be appropriate for you and for your level of understanding. Choosing to embark upon the inner journey requires courage, letting go, and an open mind. This leap of faith is exemplified in a story that Joseph Campbell recounts, describing the advice given by a Native American elder to a young initiate. *"As you go the way of life, you will see a great chasm. Jump. It is not as wide as you think."*

When Fear Enters

To illustrate this section on fear, I am going to share some of my own imagery. The following inner journey occurred for me during pregnancy. The presence of fear and the transformation of fear (through honesty, acceptance and patience) into understanding are particularly evident in this imagery:

"I am in a small boat in the sea. The blue-green water is all around me. I am feeling very secure in the boat, feeling that this imagery portrays the carrying of my unborn child. Just as the boat carries me upon the sea, I carry the child within the amniotic waters of my womb. This message is coming to me from the boat, telling me that the boat holds me like a womb holds a child. Suddenly then, the energy of the imagery shifts, and I feel a great movement beneath the boat as it lifts out of the water.

I see the form of a huge whale emerging beneath the boat, and the timbers of the boat begin to give way. I feel a terrible sense of panic and fear for my unborn child. My mind takes over, and I think this imagery may be prophetic and something awful is going to happen to wrench the child from my womb. I choose, at this point, to draw on trust and stay with the imagery. I speak my fears to the imagery itself. I tell the sea, the boat, and the whale that I am afraid for my child. I ask them what they are trying to tell me. I can almost consciously feel the place where I store the fear and breathe into the silent suspense as I wait for a reply. The boat breaks and I am in the sea. The whale is as big as a ship. It is beneath me. I sense it rising to support me. Slowly it arranges its great mass beneath me, and we move as one toward the sea's surface. I feel breath crowd my lungs as I break through to air. Something stirs me deeply and I begin to weep. I don't know why I am crying, but I let it happen.

The whale stays under me. It speaks to me then about the great movements of life, of how these movements are stronger than the forms that we build to contain our lives. It tells me that the great movements of life are supported and that I must learn to give way to them, not fighting, but embracing them and holding on, riding them to where they take me, trusting life. Whale takes me to shore. He asks me to stay close to this place that is the shore, the transition place, the defining line that divides and unites land and sea. I feel a great peace and relief; a huge welling of the mystery of creation rises in me. My hands go to my belly where my baby grows, and I cry again; this time I know why. The tears come because I am part of something that is so much greater than me, and my body sheds tears as a way of expressing and receiving this teaching."

I share this story so that you can see how fear can enter a journey. I could have abandoned the imagery when the fear entered, and I would have been left with the fear. The imagery itself took the fear and transformed it. I was left with only gratitude.

The fear of the unknown is a natural fear. In sharing this imagery story, I have illustrated the fact that you can learn to navigate fear in the waters of the inner world and glean the learning and treasure that are offered for you in that place of transformation. My intent in the writing of this book is to offer instruction for building a container (the "recipe") that can hold whatever your imagery offers you, even if that includes fear.

Working with fear can be a very genuine deterrent. For some people the belief in the power of inner images is so strong that they do not even want to look inside for fear they will create an image that will be unhealthy or dangerous for them. The truth is, our minds are creating images and chatter all the time, and not within the protected arena in which imagery is done (a space and time set aside and protected with prayer and intention to access inner knowing). The images that arise to meet us from within imagery are from the place of our innocent wholeness. They can be engaged and conversed with, and they can become our teachers as we seek to know who we are. If you fear an image that comes to you or fear that you have created this image from mind alone, tell that to the image! Speak truly; allowing yourself to feel what is motivating your fear or discomfort. Are fear and discomfort coming from a feeling of powerlessness, of being unprepared, overwhelmed, or threatened? Tell the imagery what you are truly feeling. See what it has to say! When you are face to face with the discomfort of fear within the imagery, remember to breathe. You can consciously breathe into the specific fearful images. This will help you to stay with what is happening and move you through fear to the place where it can be worked with and transformed.

Many people are confused and frightened by images that seem scary or threatening. This response is a very difficult obstacle in imagery. It is always within the menu of options to say "stop," to pass, to not look. My experience with frightening images has taught me that this path will not solve anything or make the energy that is behind the frightening image dissipate. Rather, the fear will go "on hold", waiting to be worked with at another time and in another way. Your deep self will not offer an image with which you are not strong enough to work. Your deep self holds the growth and emergence of your most dear self as its greatest interest. It will not steer you toward destruction.

If you are able, the straightest way to work with a frightening image is to befriend it (This was exemplified in the relationship with Whale in the imagery of the boat on the sea). The formula of "the recipe", here given, is big and strong enough to contain all that might emerge. It will hold your imagery. In most cases, frightening images begin to change as they are given voice and really listened to. Speak your true feelings right into the imagery. Watch what happens.

I have dealt with my own fears many times by facing them through imagery as they presented themselves. I have helped others to do the same. Sometimes the fear of fear is just too strong to allow this approach. If this is where you find yourself, you have the option of "calling in the troops" in your own imagery. You can always call a totem animal, an inner friend, or an image that represents safety and protection to be with you during your journey. In imagery you can always call for additional help. Just knowing this or having a trusted friend from the inner world there with you can help to embolden you and inspire courage to go the course of the imagery.

You may also find it useful to employ distancing when you sense fear in your imagery. Move away from the frightening image. Protect yourself from within the imagery. Converse from a place of safety. See what happens. Distancing allows you to feel safer while remaining in communication with the imagery.

When my older daughter was small, she was afraid of monsters. She would call out at night, asking "Is there a monster?" My common answer was always "No." But I wondered-- perhaps for her there was a monster? So I began doing imagery with her at this early age. One night I went to her and asked her to close her eyes and invite the monster to come forth. She bravely did this as I guided her to say "Hello" to him. I really didn't have a clue how this scenario was going to unfold and was feeling a bit unsure about pursuing this, but I held to the container of "the recipe" and "the five essential ingredients." I clearly remember what the monster told her he wanted. Popcorn! She announced this request with great clarity after asking him what he needed. In the imagery she gave him popcorn, and in fact they shared some popcorn together. Now I will not say that she never again feared monsters, but the energy of great fear seemed to dissipate following that night when a two-year old and a monster shared some imaginary popcorn.

Mistrust

Many people find it hard to trust the images that come to them. Sometimes, image after image is questioned and rejected as just being something "that I made up." My response to this common obstacle is to inquire, "Who is the 'you' that is just making this up?" As adults, we have adopted a disproportionate amount of distrust when dealing with the imagination. We have come to look upon imagination as an untamed faculty that does not deserve our respectful attention or too much consideration. When we were children, these reservations were not yet upon us, and our imaginations served as companions while life unfolded. We learned about being part of the world with the help of our imaginations. In children, the imagination is active and unbanished.

Some of the qualities of childhood can see us through life. They are not lost but perhaps just sleeping. Imagination is one of those qualities. I often encourage the person doing imagery to allow themselves the luxury of playfulness with the images, even pretending they are a child as they engage in the imagery and allow it to evolve and develop. Jesus once encouraged his followers to "...become as little children..." The place of our natural blamelessness and core truth is close to us in this place of child-like purity. Our inherant innocence is alive within us.

Over time, trust in your imagery will grow. Until this trust is built, pretend that it is there, that you trust what your inner imagery reveals to you. Be patient. Eventually, you will have the opportunity to look back at your life and actually see how you benefited from the counsel of your inner world. From that standpoint, not only will it be easier to trust the images that come to you during your imagery, but you will also notice a growing trust in the bigger picture of how imagery enhances and expands your sense of self and belonging, and thus your life and your living.

Rejection

Rejection is related to trust. Even after careful preparation and entry into your experience of imagery, rejection of the images that come can commonly occur. Many times an image is simply dismissed as being unworthy or incapable of bringing truth. When I first began doing imagery, many of my images and teachers were cartoon-like characters, even if my inquiry was deadly serious. Of course, these characters were the perfect set-up and helped me to lighten up with my imagery and to become more child-like and allowing. The tendency was often present in me, though, to reject the cartoon image for something stronger and more serious and sophisticated. "Not so," said my deeper self, as the imagery began to reveal itself through my simple acts of greeting the image (whatever it was), thanking it for coming, inquiring as to its message, and asking it what it needed and what needed to happen.

Images may also be rejected because they are given a specific point of origin in your mind. Perhaps you call for an image of prosperity, and what you see is an otter. Perhaps you have just seen a real otter in a wild setting or a zoo. Maybe you have seen a TV show or a magazine article that featured otters. You may be tempted to reject the image as one that came simply because it was close at hand in your consciousness. Think of the bank of images that lies within you as being infinite. Many images that could "work" in any given inquiry are conceivable. If a certain image is close to the surface or has been recently deposited in your internal bank of images, it is quite likely to emerge if it indeed "fits." The deeper consciousness will search until an appropriate image comes forward. Having just seen an image in physical life or the outer world is not just cause for rejecting it in the inner world.

Most people who are willing to look into their inner world through imagery are going to be receptive to the gifts that lie there. Life itself often offers experiences, encounters, and occurrences that are seen by their receivers as great gifts, as occasions for gratitude and thanksgiving. The same experiences in life are looked at differently by different people. Where one person sees opportunity another person might see only suffering. An old folk saying proclaims that one man's trash is another man's treasure. Look to your imagery with eyes that seek treasure. You will find it there.

I believe a bottom line exists in the consideration of

feelings of rejection toward your imagery, and this is it: Don't reject an image without communicating with it. Tell it that you would like to reject it. Be honest. If you persist, you will learn to accept your imagery. You will see and know the strong and powerful good medicine of the inner world. You will see where the truth of your inner world has influenced your decisions, relationships, and life. The positive effects of imagery become known to you because they are undeniable. Imagery will lead you to wonderful things, and it might be the best way there!

What your imagery offers is for you as an individual. Your imagery will show you new places of freedom, buried joy and understanding, and limitless help in diverse and very personal areas of your life. Come to it with openness and weigh what you receive on the scales of what is important. Let yourself decide whether imagery is a valuable undertaking. Does it enrich your life? Does it offer you new understandings? Does it make you freer?

Loss of Focus

For some people the task of quieting the mind is monumental. You probably know this about yourself if you are one of these people. Although it may sound incongruous, you may find having another task for your mind at the same time that you are doing imagery can be beneficial. Music as a background for imagery can be helpful for some people. It gives your mind something to cling to, something that is separate from the imagery but not removed from it. You might also try writing your imagery in a notebook while it is happening. This necessitates a lot of entrances and exits during the imagery, but it keeps you connected with what is happening and helps some people to stay focused with their imagery. If you cannot seem to stay awake during imagery, try sitting in a straight-backed chair instead of lying down or sitting in a soft chair. Some people find that journeying with eyes open works for them. Experiment with different ways of doing the imagery until you find a way that works for you.

Even for those of you who have worked with the discipline of quieting the mind, you may, without even realizing, find yourself drifting away from the imagery. Before you know what is happening, the world of imagery has been replaced with a dinner menu, a to-do list, or general drifting. Be compassionate. This is a common. Simply return to the imagery. See whether you can tighten the form or the container. What do I mean by this?

Keep the form in mind. Keep a list of the steps right in front of you, thus creating a tightened structure in which to "hold" the imagery. Some people find that a simple drumbeat can help keep the connection with their imagery. This connection through rhythm can occur in either world, the inner or the outer. Tapes or recordings of drumbeats can be used. You can drum your own rhythm, or another can drum for you. You can move awareness to the beating of your heart. Personally, I do not use a drum for imagery, but I am often aware of a rhythmic beat just below the surface of my consciousness as I enter imagery or lead another to that land.

~

The trust that you feel for your imagery will grow as you notice how the inner and outer worlds weave through the fabric of your life, facilitating and supporting positive growth, change, and fullness.

Your imagery will support the changes that occur in you as you grow in wholeness and truth. You may not fully understand the imagery. Know, though, that it has come from within you, and if you meet it with respect and honor, it will support and guide you as life unfolds and deepens, enriching your life and filling it with the truth of your being.

Part Three

A Sampler of Deep Imagery Encounters:
People and Places
Self-Discovery
Addressing Concerns
Open-Ended Inquiry

Chapter Ten

The Focus of Your Imagery Experience

Your inner world is brimming with places, teachers, and images. All of these aspects of imagery are waiting and available to come to you if you just ask. They are there as part of your inner world, ready to help you to be who you are and to learn what you most need to know in order to be who you are destined to be. Where do you begin?

Streamlining your imagery can help you to explore different areas that call for your attention. You can choose the invitation that will fulfill your present need and approach the area that you are currently interested in addressing. In the following chapters, I will suggest ways in which you can frame an invitation so that the image itself can still be fresh and surprising, yet arise from an invitation that is tailored around what you want to learn and know.

Because imagery is so inclusive of all parts of you, you can expect an overlap between a specific request and what needs to happen for your own well-being and growth. For example, you may call for an image that would represent a certain relationship, but if a pressing inner need exists of which you are unaware, such as the need for more time to play or travel, this need will probably find its way into the imagery. Conversely, if you call for who or whatever needs to come forth and are silently holding a big question about relationships in your psyche, that question will most likely be addressed at some point in the imagery, even if you don't ask about it specifically.

When you call for images, and they come, you can apply the "recipe" to assist your conversation, even if the images that present themselves are not beings. In other words, you can "speak" to a color or a feeling. You can "listen" to a stone. You can converse with landscapes and objects as well as with people, animals, and plants. I suggest that any image that comes should be treated as a guest. This hospitality will lay the groundwork for deepened communication.

The images that come to you are not static. They will change. Some images stay present in your imagery for many years or perhaps a lifetime. But mostly, images change as do people and associations in your life. Different teachings are appropriate at different times in your life. Sometimes a familiar image will come but with subtle differences. Sometimes whole new images will replace old ones. Images alter as energy changes.

You can be with the images that come to you through conversation alone, but many other ways of communication are also possible. Some people have a physical sense of their imagery, and touch is a big part of how they experience the images that come to them. Proximity can change within the imagery. You may notice yourself being very close to an image, or giving yourself plenty of distance. You may also choose to be closer or farther away. This flexibility can be a good strategy when you are unsure about an image.

In certain instances, an image will invite you to merge with it. Be sure to check this out within yourself. Is this okay with you? Through merging, you become one with the given image. You experience sight, sensation, thinking, and hearing through the senses of that image. Things that are not normally possible can become easy, things such as flying through the air or breathing comfortably under water. Vision and hearing often change during merging, creating a wonderful way to feel the image in a visceral way. When merging does occur in imagery, make certain you separate from the image before you return to the physical world unless the imagery suggests otherwise. This check-back assures closure in the inner world and smooth transition as you travel between the worlds.

In the following pages of this book, I will offer suggestions for ways to work with different styles of imagery invitations. These suggestions can be changed to reflect your personal style. The listing here is by no means complete. The possibilities for invitation are endless and can be formulated in response to personal need and desire. The ideas I offer here are based on my own personal experience with my own imagery and the imagery of those with whom I have worked. Choose what most appeals to you or try them all. May your journeys lead you to the wholeness that you seek.

PEOPLE AND PLACES

Chapter Eleven
Special Place

I begin with what I call "special place" for a reason. When you are first learning to do imagery, working with special place will help you to open your inner senses. The different aspects of place hone your awareness of the uniquely personal style of your imagery and the ways in which it comes to you. Special place imagery is powerful in and of itself, but it also helps to prepare you for further imagery by setting the stage for more imagery and enlivening your inner senses.

The place where you are, be it landscape or physical environment, plays an important role in your ability to feel connection with peace, life, and Spirit. For ages, people have made pilgrimages, going to places where they can deepen their awareness of their own true nature and their connection with Spirit. People leave their surroundings to go to other surroundings, to vacation, to see new things, and to expand beyond their ordinary boundaries. A vacation or pilgrimage to an inner place can offer the same shift in perspective and gift of refreshment.

Special place imagery offers you an anchor in your inner world, a place where you can go and become familiar, and a place you can carry within you that is always near and always available. Special place imagery offers you a place where you can feel safe, centered, and connected, no matter what is happening in the outer world.

When you embark on the special place journey, three qualities need to be affirmed as you ask for the special place to show itself to you, as you invite it to come forth. The place should feel safe. It should feel good, and it should be a place where you love to be.

When a place does not feel safe, deep instinctual feelings about survival and fear are activated. Little can happen there in the way of inner movement, growth, and learning unless the place is made to feel safe. Include the quality of safety in your request for special place.

Another important quality of a special place is that it be a place where you feel good. This aspect is very individual. What feels good to one person may not feel good to another.

I once spoke with a counselor who was exploring the use of guided imagery with her clients. She guided others by using the image of a forest. For this particular counselor, a forest was a safe and beautiful place, a place where she felt good. This counselor was working with a young female client who had suffered childhood sexual abuse. She had the client imagine herself in a green forest. Images are powerful, and it so happened that some of her client's early abuse had happened in a forest. Working with this image was neither helpful nor appropriate for this young woman since the forest was not safe for her and was not a place where she felt good or loved to be.

The counselor told me afterwards that she never again used guided imagery in her counseling. This true story illustrates the importance of allowing the imagery to come from within, of allowing your individual psyche to construct the image of special place instead of allowing the special place to be chosen by an outside source.

Here are some things to keep in mind as you prepare to call forth a special place from within. The place that comes to you may well be a place that you recognize or a place that is familiar to you in the physical world. This is fine. It may also be a place that is new, a place where you have never been in physical reality. This is also fine. Allow the place to reveal itself to you. Don't plan it.

Sometimes, you may feel bombarded with images, with many places vying for your attention! When a situation such as this develops, acknowledge the plenitude and invite a single image to come forward with clarity. Some people visit the same inner place time and time again, but for others the place is always different. Either is okay. Accept what comes to you. Stay with it. The imagery will increase in focus and dimension as you allow it to reveal itself to you.

As the image comes to you, you can call it into deeper clarity by asking yourself sensory questions. This approach is akin to focusing a camera. It draws your imagery nearer to you.

Here are some questions that recruit the inner senses and bring you more fully into your special place.

- What are the sounds of this special place?
- What are the colors that you notice around you?
- What time of day or night is it?
- What is the temperature of the air against your skin?
- What feelings are brought forth by this place?
- Where are you in this place?

When your special place is present in your mind's eye, in your imagery, use the "recipe" to go deeper. Treat the place as the guest. You have invited it. Thank it for coming. Ask it whether it has a message for you. Sense the response. Is there anything it needs? What needs to happen? Sometimes, special-place imagery can be used as a jumping-off place for more imagery to happen. From your special place you can invite an inner friend or an inner healer to come forth. Sometimes, another being will be present in your special place, and you can open dialogue with them by asking the questions you know to ask (the five essential ingredients of the "recipe"). At other times, the image of special place is a journey in itself, a place where you can be restored. An important question to consider in your special place is "How do I feel here?" Oftentimes, the feeling you are given by a place becomes the gift of the imagery.

Examples of situations where special place imagery may be helpful include those times of anxiety when you recognize a need to stay calm and intact with your inner resources, such as during medical procedures, performances, tests, or during any situation where you feel yourself hurtling away from your calm center. Another practical use of special place imagery involves going to your special place when you have a decision to make. When you are in the special inner place, all your inner resources are available to you. From this inner place the whole world of imagery is close at hand. Clarity strengthens because of the change and heightening of perspective that occurs as imagery aligns you with your true nature, and new light is shed upon the situation at hand.

Restful and restorative, special place imagery can become a mini-vacation. Many people like to bring something home with them when they are away on vacation. This souvenir-seeking activity is effective in the inner world too. Perhaps you will receive a quality such as peace, or a sense such as that of being held, or a particular object that comes as a gift from your special place. These are just a few examples where many exist. Almost certainly, your special place will offer you something that will brighten your life in the physical world. Find out what it is. Receive its gift to you.

Some Special Place Imagery Stories

The following special place story belongs to Daniel. He is 59 and has a successful career in the world of finance. He began a long and rewarding relationship with his imagery as he explored some serious health issues. His first "journey" was to a special inner place where he could feel safe and good. The place that came to him in his imagery was a place that actually existed. Here is his imagery:

"I am at the Springs. I sense the big spring water all around. I am aware of the live oak trees, the flowers, and the birds. Everything is very green. Peace and quiet permeate this place. I see turtles, snakes, and exotic birds. The air is warm and peaceful.

"I am sitting on the ground, beside the spring. I am very aware of the grass and trees. I see gray Spanish moss in the trees. The water is clear and silvery. The trunks of the trees are a rich brown color. The quiet, warmth, and peacefulness seem to seep into my bones. I have the strong feeling that life is good. Everything here is well taken care of. This includes the land and the animals."

Daniel used his special place imagery as a jumping-off place for further imagery that supported his growth and well-being in the face of a serious illness. He continues to use imagery on a regular basis as a support to his belief in the mind/body connection and his returning health.

*

Lorraine is 71. She is moving from a place that she has loved and called home for many years. As she closes her eyes and invites her "special place" to reveal itself to her, she sees herself in her own back yard. This is what her imagery shows her:

"It's summer. I'm reclining on a chaise lounge on the moss covered patio. Birds are singing. I smell earth and rocks and feel a gentle breeze. My eyes are closed and then opened to see which bird is chirping at me! I look straight up into another layer of space. It's a green canopy of beech tree leaves, one branch over another, so thick that only little spots of heavenly blue sky can be seen. It's the world of the birds --- their meadow under a blue sky."

Following her imagery, Lorraine tells me that she is considering taking this imagery with her when she makes her planned move to a new home. Even though she will be living elsewhere, this imagery will live within her for the rest of her life, connecting her with a place that she dearly loves.

*

Don is 49 and the owner of a retail business. He has been diagnosed with cardiac arrhythmia (irregular heartbeat) and has undergone a full medical work-up with treatment. He feels that stress might be a factor in his condition and wonders whether imagery could be helpful. His work with special place precedes some exploration of stress recall which leads him to the awareness that he does not breathe fully in times of stress. Here is his special place imagery:

"I am in my own bedroom, lying on my bed. The window is open, and a summer breeze fills the room. I hear the sound of the breeze. The air is soft and clean. My room looks exactly as it really looks. I am relaxed. My breathing is even and regular. My mind is alert but at rest. I feel the bed supporting the weight of my body. I relax into this support."

Don combined this special place imagery with the breathing practice of deep abdominal breathing as he explored ways to work with stress. He used imagery as an adjunct to the medical treatment he received. (Note-- in abdominal or diaphragmatic breathing, your abdomen expands during inhalation as your diaphragm lowers, allowing space for full inhalation. On exhale, your abdomen contracts toward your spine as the diaphragm returns to position, supporting complete exhalation or emptying of the lungs.)

Your Special Place Imagery

1. Protect the space. Pray.
2. Quiet your mind; relax your body (earth-air-breath-body).
3. Imagine yourself in a place that feels safe and good, a place where you love to be.
4. Open your inner senses to the world of your imagery with questions such as these:
    - Are you aware of sounds?
    - Are you aware of color?
    - What time of day or night is it?
    - What is the temperature of the air?
    - What kind of feelings are you experiencing here?
    - Where do you see yourself in this scene? Where would you like to be?

    (Go ahead and move to where you'd like to be.)
5. Allow gratitude to move out to the special place. Thank the place for revealing itself to you.
6. Ask whether this place has a message for you.
7. Does this place need anything from you? Ask.
8. How do you feel in this place? Is there more for you to know about this feeling?
9. Does anything need to happen here?
10. Is there a gift from this place that you'd like to bring out into your life with you?
11. Thank the place and say good-bye in a way that feels appropriate for you. (If further imagery is taking place, such as inquiries about decisions or invitations for other beings to be present, just continue with what comes next and thank the place for coming when the imagery is closing.)
12. Take time to fully adjust to the outer world (breath-body, earth, sky).
13. Record your journey.
14. Create ways to integrate your journey.

Chapter Twelve

Inner Friend

When you engage your imagery and invite a friend to come to you from within your deepest self, you are requesting the presence of an inner companion who can help, guide, and accompany you. I will refer to this inner being as your "inner friend."

You may have had an imaginary friend when you were a child. Many of us did. Usually this inner friend had a name and a distinct personality and appearance. The beauty of this type of friendship does not have to be confined to childhood. Throughout history men and women have been helped and encouraged by companions from the inner realms. Eminent Swiss psychologist and inner-work pioneer Carl Jung speaks of wandering in the garden while talking with his inner friend, Philemon. They had many discussions together, and Jung held their friendship in high regard.

Working with the idea of an inner friend is a versatile approach to imagery and one that can support you as you enter into other forms of imagery. Many words can be used to call forth the inner friend, and the words that you use can help to clarify the kind of friend you are calling. This inner friend can be called inner advisor, inner helper, inner counselor, or inner ally. Use a name that resonates for you. In calling forth your inner friend, you are inviting an inner being who carries the qualities of a friend, a being you know and like, a being that knows you and has your best interests at heart. I would also suggest adding the adjective "wise" to your request, for when you call forth a wise friend; you are calling forth an inner-realm companion who can offer advice and assist in your behalf on many levels.

As in all imagery, this friend may take any form, even the formless form offered by inner senses other than vision, senses such as inner hearing, inner sensing, and inner feeling. Trust what comes. Oftentimes, when you call forth a wise inner friend and engage in a conversation, you are establishing the groundwork of a lasting relationship.

Think about friendships in life. What is required to sustain them? Some attributes that come to mind are kindness, consistency, authenticity, and honesty. Some form of time spent together establishes the friendship, and time is spent getting to know one another. This time of getting to know one another is also very individual in quality. Different friendships yield different ways and styles of being together. Some are characterized by immediate affection; some are built on play and adventure, and some center upon conversation levels ranging from light to intimate. These examples are just a sampling. The style of friendship that evolves for you and your inner friend will depend on who you are and who comes to you from your inner world.

Journeying To Meet the Inner Friend

Trust needs to be established for the inner friendship to be effective. You can ask the image that comes forth whether it is indeed your inner friend and whether it has your best interests at heart. Use the "recipe" (and specifically the five essential ingredients) to establish the basic rapport and then feel free to ask anything that will make the relationship real for you. I like to ask, "What needs to happen to deepen our friendship?" This question allows the inner world, not you, to set the tone for what is needed.

Having an inner-world friend or ally with whom you have an established relationship can cut through the work of establishing a friendship or relationship every time you turn inward. Your friendship is already well established. You already know one another. Your inner friend is available to you in a moment's notice. You know this being. You can carry a sense of your friend with you in your life without going deeply into imagery. For this level of awareness to occur, you must spend time with and get to know your inner friend. Frequent inner-world imagery and spending time together in your imagery yields a deep level of friendship and support with your inner friend.

Contact with the inner friend happens in many ways. You might have an imagery "date," time you have set aside for the purpose of meeting with your inner friend. Perhaps a certain event or group of events will make you feel like you need to talk with a friend. A little quiet time alone is all you need to have that talk on an inner level. The border times of falling asleep or awakening are ripe occasions for imagery. Another nice ritual involves checking in with your inner friend on days of importance, such as birthdays, anniversaries, and days that are special to you in other ways.

Perhaps you will develop relationships with several inner friends. Usually though, a special friendship develops over time as you meet with the same familiar figure from the inner world. Again, trust what comes. Your inner friend could just as easily be an angel or a cartoon-like duck. Your inner friend is commonly present in other kinds of imagery exploration as a support and companion, and can be called for when you are stuck or confused in your imagery.

Take the time to make a friend, or friends, in the inner realm. Just as friendships in the physical world bring joy and fullness to your life, friendships in the inner world accompany you throughout your life with a treasure-trove of support, assistance, and companionship.

Some Examples of Inner Friend Imagery

Sharon is a deeply spiritual person in her late fifties. Her children are grown. She has found her way to health after many years of suffering with a chronic illness. She first met her inner friend while doing imagery with a group and then met privately with him many times.

"Bear comes to me in a sun-dappled forest. I am immediately aware of his strength and his animal nature. He is over six feet tall, and his fur is deep brown. He exudes a clean animal smell, which I find comforting. The amazing quality that encompasses him is love. He is soft and warm and full of love. We greet each other with a wonderful hug.

"Although Bear is so loving, I notice some sorrow in him and feel compassion coming from him. He tells me that he will be with me during the times of sorrow that lie ahead for me. He tells me that although painful, the times of darkness that lie ahead will precede a time that will be more wonderful than any other time of my life. I am concerned by his words "times of darkness," and I tell him this. His beautiful spirit shines so brightly as he offers me his strength and courage. He assures me that I will get through the upcoming time of sorrow, and he holds forth the promise of a bright tomorrow that will follow this coming darkness."

Sharon often met privately with Bear after this initial imagery. They would sit together on the sun-dappled forest floor. She would lean back against him, and his arms would encircle her while she absorbed his strength, love, and power. The dark period did come. Her mother had a stroke which left her right side paralyzed. Eight months later, her husband was diagnosed with a serious form of lymphoma. A year later her oldest son died.

Sharon visited her mother almost every day until her

mother's death. Her husband is in remission and is doing well. Sharon describes herself as "not out of the woods yet," but things have eased up considerably for her. She characterizes Bear as her "inner courage, strength, and power." She believes that he came to her as an amazing friend, to help her through her difficult time of grief, loss, and change, and usher her into her bright tomorrow.

*

Rona is 40. She has long been interested in the body-mind-Spirit connection, and has used imagery before, although she has never journeyed inward specifically to find a friend or inner companion. Here is her inner friend journey:

"As I close my eyes, I see a little monk doll that I had as a girl. It is a home-made doll, and it wears a brown robe with a hood. The face has painted dots for the eyes and nose, and the doll has a beard made of soft wool. I say "hello" to it, and it seems to become real. I am at the sea. I am sitting on a bench, and a man in a coarse brown robe sits beside me. He tells me that his name is Brother David. He looks like a combination of Sean Connery and my grandfather. I trust him and tell him this. He touches my face and tells me I am fine. As we look out to sea, I feel him take my hand. His hand is weathered, and his skin feels rough and warm. I notice his clean, short nails as our joined hands rest on my lap.

"I tell Brother David that I have struggled with feeling waywardness in my heart. My home and family are dear to me, but my heart wants so much more. He tells me to name the things I want, to write them in the sand. As I begin to write, he asks me when I will run out of room. I consider this question as I look at the long span of beach that stretches in either direction. He smiles. He tells me not to worry. He tells me that my heart can hold more than I can imagine. I ask him what he needs from me. He bows his head. When he looks at

67

me again, he says, "Tomorrow." I sense he means more than just another meeting. I sense we will be together for a long time. I nod my head and answer, "Tomorrow." I feel something move in me, as though something has shifted. I have made a commitment I will honor, and I will return to this bench with him many times for many visits, with many questions. I sense I have found a lifetime companion."

Years after this initial meeting, Rona still names Brother David as her inner friend. She says that they have times of conversation as well as times of silence, sitting on the bench together or walking on the beach. She goes to him when she is confused, troubled, or in need of advice. She also says she goes inward to visit with him for the pure joy of being with him. On a practical note, she reports a feeling of greater stability and a new willingness to trust what is happening in her life since she has met and befriended her inner friend, Brother David.

Your Inner Friend Imagery

1. Protect the space. Pray.
2. Quiet your mind; relax your body (earth-air-breath-body).
   (Optional) Go to your inner "Special-Place".
3. Call out and ask your inner friend to come and be with you. Use any terminology that resonates for you (ex: inner counselor, inner helper, or inner ally).
4. Enter into a conversation using the five essential ingredients.

   > Ingredient 1- Greet the image. Thank it for coming.
   >
   > Ingredient 2- Ask the image whether it comes with a message for you.
   >
   > Ingredient 3- Ask the image whether it needs something from you.
   >
   > Ingredient 4- Ask whether anything else needs to happen.
   > (Optional) Ask your inner friend whether there is anything that can happen to deepen your relationship with each other.
   >
   > Ingredient 5- Thank your inner friend, and say "good-bye."

5. Take your time to adjust fully to the outer world (breath-body-earth-sky).
6. Record your journey
7. Create ways to integrate your journey.

Chapter Thirteen
The Inner Chapel

People need a place where they can feel peace and rest and where they can be close their God, a place of divine presence where questions can be asked, and decisions can be made; a place where the outpouring of grief or joy and the turnings of the human heart can be literally or metaphorically placed on the altar and brought before God; a place where they can feel a special closeness with the God who made them. Prayers can take many forms, and mankind has found many ways to come close to God. Imagery is one beautiful way of experiencing spiritual communion.

A place that welcomes and is conducive to prayer can deepen your sense of prayer. A stunning vista, a shining lake, a meadow of wildflowers or a wild, lonely place can help us feel close to the mystery of God. Closeness to nature helps most people to feel close to God.

Some people are fortunate enough to have actual places in their lives that welcome this closeness. For some it is a hilltop or a riverbank, for others it is a church or a favored room. For some, this place that inspires reverence is far enough away that frequent visits are difficult and this place is real in memory only. Everyone carries their inner world with them wherever they go, and inside you is a place, perhaps many places, where prayer can deepen and you can feel a renewed closeness with God.

The late Jesuit teacher and author Anthony De Mello

teaches that one of the finest helps to prayer is a place that is conducive to prayer. He speaks of how a starry night or a beautiful dawn or twilight can deepen our sense of closeness to God, and therefore deepen our prayers. He suggests that we need to expose ourselves long and lovingly to the places that help us pray, and he adds that these places can be carried in our hearts and etched in our memories, where we can return to them time and time again in our imagery

I have called this imagery exercise the "Inner Chapel." The word chapel is derived via Old French *chapele* and medieval Latin *capella*, meaning "small hooded cloak." It denotes a covering for the head. This covering invokes the lightest sense of a personal shelter. The definition of chapel is a place of worship. It usually has its own altar, intended for private prayer. It is not necessarily a church. The derivations and meanings of the word "chapel" come together to create an impression of protection and intimacy. The word itself stirs the feeling sense.

In preparation for working with inner chapel imagery, think back on places where you have felt especially close to God. Even if the place is one of great vastness, it can become a candidate for the inner chapel. It is simply a place where you feel very close to God, a place where you can bare your soul.

Doing Inner Chapel Imagery

Take some time to prepare for the imagery. Become quiet and relaxed. Ideally you are in a place that is relatively free from distraction. Allow your heart and mind to turn toward what you are doing. Offer any prayers that you'd like to accompany your going within. As you settle into the place where imagery happens for you, ask that your inner chapel reveal itself to you. Let it come in its own

time. Sometimes several images will come and then blend
into one, or one will just get stronger and clearer as the
others fade. This place may be an image that came to mind
when you considered places where you felt close to God. It
may also be a place that is totally new to you and which
emerges from your imaginative depths, from the deep well
that is within you and embraces all that you are.

As this place, this inner chapel, reveals itself to you,
take time to notice the general landscape. Are you inside
or outside? If you are outside, are you aware of structures,
buildings, or similar shelters? If you are inside, are you
aware of what lies beyond the building itself; are you part
of a greater landscape? Act naturally. What would you do
if you were at this place in physical life? Would you look
around a bit? Go ahead and do that. Notice everything.
See the place as vividly as you can. See the colors. Hear
the sounds. Feel the quality of the air and the light. Are
you aware of smells? Do you notice an altar, a place of
special meaning? Is a prayer living in your heart that
wants to be raised to God? Go ahead and do that. Take
your time. Open your heart to prayer.

Perhaps you would like just to be here in this place.
Give yourself that freedom. Does something need to
happen? There are countless ways of being in your inner
chapel. Perhaps you'd like to light a candle, assume a
certain posture, or become active here in some way.
Perhaps you long for stillness. Notice your inclinations.
Follow them. In the world of imagery all things are
possible. Pray here in your own way. Allow the imagery
to unfold.

Sometimes, you will be joined by another being,
perhaps a beloved Master from your tradition, an angel or
an animal. Stay open. If you would like the presence of
another, you can offer that invitation. I have seen many be
joined by Jesus, by angels, or by loved ones (living and
deceased) as they did this exercise. Remember not to force

or choreograph what occurs. Invite. Allow. Perhaps active dialogue, silent heartfelt dialogue, or deep silence will be a part of your time in your inner chapel.

If you have a question or a problem that you would like to leave in this place, you can do that. You then leave with the knowledge that your question or concern is being held in this sacred space while you carry on simultaneously with your life. This is your place and you are welcome here. You may return as often as you like.

As your visit in your inner chapel draws to a close, bid any others there with you good-bye, as well as the place itself. If you'd like to leave a gift or offering there, do so in a way that feels right to you. Give thanks. Breathe. Gradually let your awareness return to the physical world and to your presence in your body.

If you can, give yourself a little quiet time before going immediately back into the activities of your life. A walk or a bath or even work that is done with your hands will ease the transition and honor the journey. Receive the blessing of the time you have spent in your inner chapel. You carry it with you wherever you go, and it is available to you whenever you need it.

The image of your inner chapel, or prayer shelter, can be used when you need to quickly center yourself in God. You may choose to use the image as a constant reminder by keeping it etched in your mind as you go about your days. The image you find is there for you. If you choose, you can bid it to imprint its reflection in your mind, heart, and body, where it will be a consistent refuge for you.

Inner Chapel Stories

As a guide, I have been deeply touched by this simple practice and the beauty of the worlds that have opened for those who have made these journeys. I will begin with my own inner chapel story. The peace I have received in this place is the inspiration that led me to share this practice with others.

"I am in a high place. The sky is blue with moving clouds. The land itself is like a field. The grasses are golden and tall. A small building is to my left. It is framed with wood. Inside the building are two simple benches. A spring flows from the ground. Beside the spring is a round stone cover. The altar is of stone. A small alcove nests beside it. A candle burns in red glass against the wall. A round window of stained glass mosaic faces me. A plain door with metal latchwork leads from the side of the building to the outdoors. The air is rarefied.

"This is a place of deep rest. Often, when I am here, I am aware of the presence of my Lord. Sometimes, we lie down together in the tall grass and watch the clouds. I feel my heart, joyful and awake, resting."

I find that if I go to this place in my imagery, I feel freer in my prayers. I also sense a deeper connection with Jesus, who often joins me in this prayer place. This is not the only way that I pray, but it is a beautiful way.

*

The story that follows belongs to Sean. He is 46, a physician who works in public health serving a large metropolitan region. Here is the inner chapel story that he shared with me:

"I close my eyes and pray, "Take me to my inner chapel." I am instantly in an unexpected place. I am on the beach along a short inlet that connects out past its gate with the beautiful sea. The gate is narrow with steep rock walls.

"I stand in a cove. The water is shallow. As I look out at the blue water, I sense a glowing eminence that is the source of everything coming from the water. It is God. The water extends into my inlet and is clear, warm, and alive. I bathe in it and feel its refreshing love and energy flow through my skin into my reality. I feel the presence of a friend. Then I see another brilliant living Being coming from around the other side of the inlet. I feel this must be Jesus. I find a place where we can sit on some warm rocks by the water. He comes and sits directly across from me. As I hold his hands, a great sadness flows away from me, and his love flows in.

"He indicates that our time together is complete. I make a fire on the rocks, behind a lovely rock where I can sit and look across the inlet to the sea. I notice a dense forest bordering the beach, and I realize it is a limitless source for maintaining my fire. The spot where I have built the fire is my altar. As long as it is needed, I will never let the fire go out."

After sharing this story, Sean also shared these observations: "In every way, my little chapel is the perfect place for me. It is the perfect retreat for learning. It is my private window to and with God."

*

The following inner chapel story belongs to John. He is 65 years old and a school bus driver. His story follows:

"I find myself in a wooded glen, in front of a waterfall. Behind the falls is a cave. I am aware of a teepee above the falls. Ribbons and banners of bright primary colors flutter from its poles. The colors of the landscape are greens and earth tones. Rocks sparkle with wetness on the *left side of the cave, where a candle sits atop a stone ledge. I prostrate myself before this simple altar (not something familiar to me in my daily life).*

"I see my parents here. They are young and so am I. We are all dressed in buckskins. My parents speak to me of how they appreciate me. They speak of wishing they hadn't forced me into certain things when I was young. They apologize. I am deeply moved."

John found a place of deep healing and deep emotion in his inner chapel. Tears flowed as he freely shared his imagery. He later shared with me that he revisits his inner chapel from time to time, and each time he visits there he experiences peacefulness and serenity.

*

This prayer and imagery practice is offered freely. It is a way to amplify the prayers of your heart, in the spirit of whatever tradition you embrace. Follow the simple guidelines and find your own inner chapel. If you repeat the practice frequently, it will become second nature to you. May your journeys be blessed.

Doing Inner Chapel Imagery

1. Protect the space. Pray.
2. Quiet your mind. Relax your body (earth-air-breath-body).
3. Ask inwardly that your inner chapel reveal itself to you.
4. Notice everything about your inner chapel with your inner senses.
   - Are you inside or outside?
   - What do you notice around you?
   - What are the colors, sounds, and smells of this place?
5. Are you drawn to explore this inner chapel? If so, go ahead.
6. Is there an altar of any kind here? Or a special place where you'd like to pray?
7. Open your heart to prayer, and pray here in your own way.
8. Does anything need to happen while you're here? Allow this if it feels right to you.
9. Is there an action you'd like to engage in while here? (Ex:lighting a candle, a special prayer posture, a gesture of gratitude or offering).
10. Do you have a question or problem that you'd like to leave here?
11. If you are joined here by other beings, begin a dialogue if it feels appropriate.
    - Greet them and thank them for coming.
    - Do they have a message for you?
    - Is there something they need from you?
    - What needs to happen?
    - When you are ready, thank them and say good-bye.

12. Thank your inner chapel for revealing itself. Say good-bye.
13. Record your journey.
14. Give yourself time for integration. Be with the energy of your journey. (ex: Take a walk, do work with your hands, spend some quiet time alone).

Self-Discovery

"Ask the animals, and they will teach you, or the birds of the air, and they will tell you; or speak to the earth, and it will teach you, or let the fish of the sea inform you."
The Book of Job 12: 7-8

Chapter Fourteen
Animal Imagery

Human beings are one of many life-forms on Earth. For myriad creatures of all types and plants of amazing variety, this planet is home. In the depths of the human mind there lies an awareness and knowledge of the other life forms with which we share our planet. Some of these other life forms we have seen with our own eyes as we observe them in their natural environments. Others we have domesticated, and with them we share our lives and sometimes our living rooms. Some we have seen on the screens of televisions and in magazines and books. Sometimes we fear them or consider them a nuisance. Their presence among us is our daily fare. We are fascinated by them. Children love them. A school librarian once told me that the books most borrowed by children are the books about animals. The native people of America called the animals brother and sister, as did Francis, the beloved saint from Assisi, who is known for his love of them.

In the Native American tradition, a pervasive respect and sense of kinship tied human relationship with that of plants and animals. I will use the teachings of Lakota Chief Luther Standing Bear of the Teton Sioux to illustrate this belief in the relatedness of all beings. Chief Standing Bear spoke of the unifying life force that flowed in and through all things. This life force was believed to have been breathed into the first human, thus uniting all things in kinship within the Great Mystery. This belief was active, uniting the human being with the flowers, the blowing winds, the rocks, the trees, and the animals. This belief manifested in the people as an abiding love, joy, and reverence for the mystery of life where all of existence held a sacred place.

Kinship with other beings has a place deep in the human psyche. Animals and plants come as visitors in your dreams and imagery. They speak to you of parts of yourself that are primal and instinctual. Within imagery, the energies inside you that are coming to expression can take the form of these brothers and sisters of the plant and animal kingdoms. Nature offers a host of forms from which the sub-conscious may choose. This is the realm of animal imagery. The animals inside you can teach and guide you and help you return to the joy and mystery of living your truth.

My Background with the Animals

In my first experience with doing deep imagery, I met and worked with Eligio Stephen Gallegos, who is affectionately known by his students as Steve. The work that Steve was offering at that time was imagery which focused on the chakras or energy centers of the body. The concept of chakras is ancient and comes to us from India. Chakra means "wheel" in Sanskrit. Each chakra (we'll look at a system that identifies eight of them) corresponds to a specific location and region of consciousness in the body, where these "wheels" of energy relate to different aspects of your being. The chakras, or wheels of energy, are located in ascending order at the base of the spine, the belly, the solar plexus (between navel and heart), the heart, the throat, the forehead, the top of the head or "crown", and an area about 5-8 inches above the head, known as the transpersonal chakra. Steve invited a group of us to close our eyes and invite the animals of the various chakras to come to us in our imagery. We focused on a specific chakra while he led us to ask its' representative animal to come forth. He used a pattern of communication with the animals that I teach in this book and have called the "recipe." He now carries this work around the world. I became a student of the "animal work", as it is called by those who live and work with it. It is a simple and wonderful way to learn the rhythms of your own imagery while at the same time exploring varied aspects of your being as you change and grow in wholeness and truth.

The Chakra Animals

The animals can be called upon in many types of imagery inquiry. Calling for an animal is a clear and direct invitation that narrows down the infinite possibilities of imagery. For example, it is very clear to say, "Animal of my heart, will you come forth?" It is also possible to say, "Image from my heart, will you come forth?" Both questions offer infinite possibility, but calling for the animal is more direct and this makes the process and the invitation a bit more succinct. Whichever you choose, remember to greet whatever it is that you see. If you have called for an animal and what you see is a canoe, then you greet the canoe!

Working with the chakra (pronounced chäk'-rä) animals is a wonderful introduction to doing imagery. Here is a simple way to proceed: Following preliminaries outlined in the "recipe," you protect the space, pray, quiet your mind, and relax your body. Then allow your focus to come softly to the chakra with which you are working. Call out silently from inside, inviting the animal of the chakra with which you are working to come forth. Greet it, and thank it for coming. Ask it whether it has come with a message for you or with something to show or tell you. Allow the story to unfold. Travel with the animal, speak with it, and look at what it shows you. Ask it what it needs. Make inquiry about what needs to happen. When there is a sense of completion, say "good-bye," and thank the animal. When your journey is complete, take some time to readjust to the physical world. Record your journey. Find some ways to integrate what you have discovered. The rhythms and energies within you have taken form and have spoken to you through your inner language of imagery. Frequently, a new aliveness is experienced as the animals reveal themselves and lead you toward insight, healing, and friendship on an inner level.

In the chakra animal work as it is taught by Steve Gallegos (The Personal Totem Pole Process™), the animals of the chakras then come together in council, entering into communication and relationship with each other. This council often becomes a place of amazing healing and change. Typically, the crown animal decides where the council will be held, and the animals of the chakras gather in this chosen spot. In council, all have an equal voice and in this place all can be heard. The conversation is allowed to unfold naturally, with each animal being given the opportunity to speak.

There is much to be discovered, and many sources are available to the reader who wants to learn more about the chakras and the work with the chakra animals. I will simply list the location of the chakras in this text, along with their most basic aspects, (although this varies according to some sources) and offer you the reader further sources in the bibliography if you wish to pursue exploration with this form of imagery or the chakras themselves.

1st chakra: located at the base of the spine, the sacrococcygeal nerve plexus, also called the root chakra. Corresponds to security, safety, and groundedness.

2nd chakra: located just below the navel in the lower abdomen, also known as the belly chakra. Pertains to feelings, fluidity, creativity, and sensuality.

3rd chakra: located at the solar plexus, between the heart and the navel. Relates to vitality, action, self-esteem, self-respect, and personal power.

4th chakra: located in and around the heart, known as the heart chakra. Focuses on love, compassion, forgiveness, and community.

5th chakra: located in and around the throat, known as the

throat chakra. Has to do with communication, truth, choice, and expression.

6th chakra: located in the forehead, also known as the "third eye", midway between eyebrows and pineal gland. Relates to intellect, intuition, wisdom, clarity, and the call to spiritual growth.

7th chakra: located at the top of the head, also known as the crown chakra. Corresponds with Spirit, grace, and divine presence.

8th chakra: located about 5-8 inches above the head, also known as the transpersonal chakra. Connects the individual with the greater universe and infinite consciousness.

An example of a chakra animal journey will be given at the end of this chapter. Even though specific qualities are ascribed to each chakra, chakra qualities can vary from individual to individual. The animals themselves will tell you about the energy of the chakra where they are found, its state of health, and its strength or weakness. This information my not be literal, but becomes evident in the imagery of that area.

The Wide Range of Animal Imagery

The animals that you meet in imagery can help you find the places in yourself where you can grow and change. They may be sick when you see them or in cages or prisons. They may be weak and in need of nourishment and support, or fighting with each other. All people are different, as are the energies that exist within them. The animals will show you your strengths and your weaknesses and help you to develop and grow in a natural way. Ask them what they need. They will tell you.

An animal can be called for in any inquiry. In my many years of guiding, animals are by far the most often seen helpers of the inner world. Perhaps you want to explore your relationships with friends. You could call for an animal of friendship. Perhaps you are being called upon to act as a leader. You could call for an animal of leadership. The animals can help to show you the gifts that you have to offer to the world. The Native Americans often used the idea of medicine animals. These were animals that denoted one's own gifts, one's own healing path, and one's connection with the mystery of life. You can call for medicine animals that are specific to certain situations or as life companions that help you grow into the fullness of your being, reminding you constantly of your strengths and your sense of purpose and being. In this aspect you are never alone because they are always with you. The animals are there inside you waiting to reveal themselves to you.

Animal Imagery Stories

The following true imagery stories illustrate some different ways to work with the animals in your imagery. In the first story, a young student of mine seeks an animal totem through imagery. The second story illustrates a healer's work with his chakra animals, and the messages he receives from them through his imagery.

Lisa is a young college student whom I first came to know as a student in my yoga class. She was interested in imagery, and scheduled an imagery session to meet with what she called her animal totem; a medicine animal that could help her feel grounded and connected to life. She wanted to deepen her connection with the earth and expressed a deep interest in Native American customs and beliefs. She was friendly and animated around people but said she often felt depressed without really knowing why. Here is Lisa's journey to meet her medicine animal:

"I call out for my medicine animal. At first, I am aware of green eyes. They are clear like deep pools. I sense a golden

cat with a long tail, a large lioness. I greet Cat and thank it for coming. It looks intently at me, a curious aliveness in its eyes. I notice its tail is softly flicking, and it has a cartoon quality one minute, a real animal quality the next. I ask whether it has come with a message for me.

"It begins to clean itself in cat-like fashion with its tongue. It is cleaning the white area of its chest. It tells me that I must do the same, that my heart must be pure for her to be its companion. I don't understand. Cat reminds me of how I avoid others, avoid situations where I might stand out, and avoid speaking from my heart because doing that might "stir things up". I become aware of my feelings of shame and inadequacy. Cat tells me that her medicine is strong and that I must wear the "badge" of a pure heart to gain her trust.

"What must I do?" I ask the cat. Cat tells me that I must turn my thoughts to courage when it is time to speak from the heart, that the words cannot be buried under feelings of shame any longer. Cat tells me that she will be always by my side. Cat tells me I can touch my own chest and remember the snowy white fur of Cat's chest and that if I can do this when it is time to speak, I will find courage and gain purity in the act of speaking from my heart.

"I ask Cat what she needs. 'I need a place to lie down.'

"I imagine a sunny spot beside a great tree. There is a great openness in the place I see and the sky is bright and full of clean air and warmth. I touch the soft earth beneath the tree and smooth a place for Cat to lie. Cat walks over, her legs strong and muscled, and shows movement in her tail as she takes her place in the bed that I have made for her. I ask Cat what needs to happen. Cat says she will be there, always, and that I should not forget her. She reaches out with her paw and touches my chest as though she were marking it with her paw print. I put my hand on the Cat's paw as I thank Cat, and we say good-bye to each other."

The lioness became Lisa's "medicine" animal. It was also the animal that came to her heart when she later journeyed to meet her chakra animals, for the cat had made a home in her heart. She had many subsequent journeys with this lioness, but this first one marked their first "meeting" and began their friendship, which continues to this day, as Lisa grows into a strong and clear young woman who speaks from her heart without shame.

*

Jeremy is 39. He is a gifted healer and massage therapist who is intrigued by the concept of chakra imagery and wants to meet his chakra animals. He has done a lot of inner work but never imagery specifically. I share his chakra imagery below:

Root Chakra: "I see a large fish. He swims through the sea with intention. I have the feeling he is blind. I greet him and ask, 'Can you see?' He shows me slits on the side of his body, and tells me this is how he observes the world around him. He takes information into his body. I ask him whether he needs anything. He wants to eat my hands. I am reluctant, and tell him so. He tells me this is a way of integrating the way I use my hands for healing. I know this might be crazy but I trust him and I allow this to happen. He tells me to imagine the lines on my palms as gills, which will help me to give and receive while working with others. I feel like he is an old friend, and I tell him this. My hands are intact even though I have allowed him to 'eat' them."

Belly Chakra: "A leopard is high in a tree. Its tail is long and curls with an up and down motion. It wants me to merge with it. When I do this, I feel the sensitivity of the long tail. The sounds of the forest are loud, nearly deafening. I feel a supreme stillness in my body. This combines with the sense of muscular potential. *I feel like I could spring with my body and pounce, jumping a half mile! As I come back to being me, I have a new appreciation of leopard. I tell it this. I ask what needs to happen. Leopard tells me to imagine myself with a tail and to imagine my tail as graceful. It tells me to hone the strength in my legs and in my body. Leopard tells me that its name is Graceful. I stroke the length of its sinuous body as we say good-bye."*

Solar Plexus Chakra: *"A large elephant stands before me. She raises her trunk in greeting. I walk up to her, and touch the leathery dry skin of her massive leg. She will go with me wherever I go. She wants me to practice talking through her mouth. I tell her I will try. She opens her mouth wide and I see the huge pinkness of the inside of her mouth. I am aware that my mouth is the same color. I tell her this. She tells me that no one suspects her of being afraid, but inside there are fears. I see two small elephants running up behind her. She raises her trunk and touches my forehead with it. She says we will visit often, and we will look at the fears together. She will also let me play with the young elephants. I thank her for her strength and beauty. I tell her I look forward to seeing her often."*

Heart Chakra: *"I see a small monkey with a large red flower. He is cartoonish, looking a bit like Curious George. I can tell he is shy, as he hides behind the flower. He tells me he is tired, and he wants to rest. He pulls a blanket over his face. I ask him to tell me about resting. He wants me to take a day off every week, to schedule no clients and to do the things I love to do, like fishing, reading, and studying new ideas. I feel a lightness when he tells me this. I tell him I will try. He is sleeping now under his yellow blanket. I thank him anyway as I say good-bye."*

Throat Chakra: "*I see this animal immediately. It is a turtle. His legs are very strong and his neck is very long. I say 'Hello.' Turtle smiles. He tells me he wants to walk, to move. He is capable of stillness but he is so determined to move right now. He wants me to move with him. I get on his back. Our pace is slow and lumbering, and this feels right to me. I can see and smell everything. I see the image of musical notes. I tell turtle this, and he says he wants me to sing as we move. He suggests I sing often, not words, but tones and humming. He asks me to do this now. (Jeremy does this.) He says that is all for now, but as I say good-bye, he tells me his name is Crag Singer, and that he is a friend of elephant who I met in my solar plexus.*"

Forehead Chakra: "*Here I see first two, and then a whole family of ground squirrels. They have a large acorn and they are all busy and chattering. Two squirrels argue over the acorn. They each want it, not to eat, but to bury and store for winter. I greet them, and thank them for showing up. I comment about the great deal of activity going on here. They are too busy to listen, and I have trouble getting their attention. A brown horse appears. The horse suggests I, too, may be too busy to listen. Horse tells me I can listen in many ways, not just with my ears, but with my whole body and my senses. I recall a scene from childhood when I was fishing with my uncle. I had cast way out into the water and hadn't had a bite. Then my uncle showed me some beautiful fish feeding right in front of us. You could see them in the water. As I remember this event, Horse lets me know that it wants me to understand and expand my own ways of gathering wisdom. He has shown me the memory so I will remember to open my eyes and look at what is in front of me. He tells me to put my hands on the acorn. He tells me to really listen. My hands move as the acorn grows and sprouts. Before long, my hands are around a magnificent oak tree, and I am awe-struck. Horse stands beside the tree. The horse and the tree are partners. They are here with me. This is enough for now.*"

Crown Chakra: "I sense the image of a golden crown, like a king would wear. It is round, with points that reach up. Red stones shine from their settings in the crown. I greet the crown and thank it for presenting itself. I ask if it has a message for me. I hear, 'You are of royal blood.' I don't understand, and tell it so. I have a sense of these words, 'you have gifts. They are your legacy. They have been passed down to you from those that came before you. Learn about them. Don't fear them.' The talking crown begins to fade. It tells me that soon I can wear it.

8th or Transpersonal Chakra: "A bird is overhead. Its wing span is huge. I sense myself riding on its back, just behind its head. I look at the ground far below and see the shadow that we make moving across the earth. The earth looks so green from up here. The water looks silver and pure. Everything sparkles with clean beauty. I feel a deep sadness that the Earth has been so changed by modern man. I tell the bird. It does not answer, but I know that what I see is the true splendor of creation. I ask the bird what it needs. Again, it does not answer, but I feel my hand being drawn to its neck, and the feathers are soft and brown. I hear it give a sharp whistle and I feel the vibration of this sound against Bird's throat which is beneath my fingers. I remember a Native American teaching about aspiring to be a hollow whistle through which the breath of the Creator can blow. As I think of this I sense myself as hollow, like a flute, with God's love pouring into and through me. I know it is time to leave. I say good-bye to this amazing bird, and feel myself back on the ground, looking up at bird's huge wing span. I wave. Again, I hear the shrill call, the whistle of bird's answer to me."

Jeremy later met with all his animals in council, which was held under the tall Oak. All were present. The large fish swam in a deep sea beneath the earth that supported the tree, and the great bird flew overhead. In council, the animals let Jeremy know that they cared deeply for him and wanted him to know that his gifts made him unique. The monkey in his heart received gifts of words, service, and affection from all the other animals and was officially welcomed into the fold during the council.

Jeremy later told me that he continues to meet with his animals and that his work with the animals has helped him to accept his true self and his unique healing skills. He spoke of how he used to be so concerned about the approval of others, not wanting them to think of him as strange. He feels that his animals have helped him to know, love, respect, and accept himself as he truly is.

Doing Animal Imagery

1. Protect the space. Pray.
2. Quiet your mind. Relax your body (earth-air-breath-body).
3. Bring your attention to your request. If you are doing chakra imagery, bring your attention to that particular location in your body. If you are calling for an animal to represent a quality (ex: friendship, leadership), focus on that quality. If you are calling for a medicine animal, focus deeply on your request.
4. Call out inwardly, inviting the animal to come forth.
5. Enter into conversation using the five essential ingredients.

     Ingredient 1- Greet the animal. Thank it for coming.

     Ingredient 2- Ask the animal whether it has a message for you, or if it has something to show you or tell you.

     Ingredient 3- Ask the animal if there is anything it needs from you.

     Ingredient 4- What else needs to happen? (Optional) Does something need to happen that can deepen your relationship with each other?

     Ingredient 5- Thank the animal for coming, and say good-bye.

6. Take time to make the transition to the outer world (breath-body-earth-sky).
7. Record your journey.
8. Create ways to integrate your journey, bringing aspects of the inner world into the outer world.

"Go to your bosom, knock there, and ask your heart what it doth know"   William Shakespeare (Measure For Measure)

Chapter Fifteen
The Heart

Your heart is a key organ of your body, active from the moment of life's beginning, endlessly receiving and giving blood to sustain and nourish all of your body's cells. It is the reservoir from which the lifeblood of your body is freshened and sent forth. Your heart uses electricity to synchronize its action. Through this process of synchronized giving and receiving (pumping), your heart reaches out and conducts the rhythms of the rest of your body. This is the physical action of your heart. Underneath this physical action, there exists a mysterious and vast inner capacity. It is the place where love is held and from which love is given. Here in the heart, we can hold those whom we love, even those far away or who are no longer with us physically. Our hearts know joy and sorrow. Our hearts are sacred containers within us, where we can hold and access feelings, memories, wishes and dreams. Our hearts know things, and have knowledge that they will share if we will listen.

Your heart lies in the center of your body where it integrates the physical part of your existence with the depths of your being. Your heart seeks to reveal itself to you if you allow this. Your heart is unlike any other heart.

Folk wisdom teaches that to be real one must come "from the heart." This link with the heart can make all the difference. The movement of your awareness to your heart can change the energy of a conversation, a project, a task, a prayer, or a day in your life. It can disassemble the constraints of time. It can infuse life with newness in its pattern of replenishing. Your heart is always present, and yet the gifts of heart energy strengthen when conscious attention is given to the presence of your heart. The spoken word will be heard and perceived differently if the person speaking consciously speaks "from the heart."

In its steadfast presence your heart reminds you that forces exist that are always present, even when your attention is turned elsewhere. Its beating continues. All you need to do to be reminded of this is to bring your hand to your heart. You will feel the beating. You will hear it if you are very quiet. It is a constant signal coming from the core of you.

Our hearts are touched in many ways and by many things. Music, art, senses, beauty, stories, experience... all these can take you deeper into your heart. Attention to your heart will deepen all your activities, but your heart offers even more than the gifts of heartful awareness. As a human, you have the opportunity to know your heart. In the deep chambers of your heart, giving and receiving become possible when you are fully present with respect and attention. Imagery is one powerful and vital way that this giving and receiving can happen.

Through the gift of imagery, I have stayed close to the movements of my own heart and have helped others to know their hearts with greater intimacy. To the reader, I give blessing to the heart journeys that lie before you. The process is simple. Try not to be discouraged if you lose your attention during the imagery. Return with patience and self-compassion. The journey is there, waiting. The "recipe" will guide you as you look within.

The Heart Journey

Prepare yourself and your space for the journey. Pray in your own way. Allow your focus to move toward your heart as you consciously make the connection with your breathing and with your body, with air and with Earth. Sense your attention coming to rest softly around your heart. Call out from inside of you, asking an image to come forth from your heart. Greet it, thank it, and engage it in conversation. "What do you have to show me or tell me?" "What do you need?" "What needs to happen?" Write the journey down. Honor it. Live with it. Give it room in your life.

There are as many ways of working with heart imagery as there are stars in the sky. You can delve into love and sorrow, health and sickness, freedom and constraint. Your heart will have its own ideas about where it wants to take you. Be patient. Visit often. If you have a strong journey, sometimes it is good to let the heart imagery "breathe;" not crowding it with other journeys right away. A neglected heart can lead to disease. This is a known fact. Less known is the fact that the attended heart will share its gifts with you. It will see you through your life with its full embrace.

Heart Imagery

Sharing My Story

The first formal imagery I ever did was heart imagery. My soon-to-be teacher was leading a workshop that introduced a body of work in which animal images were invited to come forth from the chakras, or energy centers of the body (see previous chapter). One of these energy centers is the heart, and that is where he began.

Many people sat in a circle. We were asked to focus on our hearts. He invited us to call forth an image from our hearts. What I was about to hear from my own heart was about truth and healing. This relates directly to who I am. The others in this circle heard messages that related to them as individuals. Many journeys centered on love, patience, faith, old hurts, and the presence of deep comfort. A great breadth of substance lies within the heart's domain. Here is the story of my first journey.

Things seemed blurred behind my closed eyes. I thought I saw some eyes. Eventually, I was aware of a lobster. His claw was banded with a blue rubber band which restrained him in the manner of restaurant lobsters. He seemed a bit sick. As I was

99

guided into dialogue with Lobster (this was my first experience with the dialogue formula, which I have shared as the "recipe"), *I learned from Lobster that he was sick, that he was full to gagging on something, and that he wanted me to pull it out of him. A small bit of something that looked like packing tape protruded from his mouth. I began to pull on it, and it started to come out. I pulled and pulled great piles of it, more than could have possibly fit inside him. As I pulled, it just kept coming. Finally, I was done. I asked him what it was. He told me that it was everything I had ever read, or been taught, or been fed as the truth. It was everything that had ever been "stuffed down my throat." It was making me sick. He imparted the idea that I was to come carefully to my own truth about things, that all this information from others was clogging something vital within me. He began to grow, and his color became deeper and his eyes brighter. I noticed the rubber band was no longer restraining him. He looked healthier. I thanked him and bid him good-bye.*

As I opened my eyes, things didn't seem quite real, and yet lightness was in me, as though a great cleansing had taken place. From that time I decided to weigh teachings from the place of my own inner truth. In some ways that seemed dangerous, but that is what freed me.

My first journey prepared me for all the journeys that have followed. My heart showed me that my own truth can be found within me, and that ingesting truth that is not my own will harm me. My heart animal has changed many times since this first journey, and the road that the heart takes is not always easy.... but nothing compares. My heart has shared itself with me in many ways since that first heart journey, giving life a flavor, sound, color, taste, and fragrance I could have never imagined.

Doing Heart Imagery

1. Protect the space. Pray.
2. Quiet your mind. Relax your body (earth-air-breath-body).
3. Let your focus come gently to the region of your heart.
4. Call out inwardly, inviting your heart to come to you as an image.
5. Begin dialogue, using the five essential ingredients.

> Ingredient 1- Greet the image. Thank it for coming.
>
> Ingredient 2- Ask the image if it has a message for you, something to show you or tell you.
>
> Ingredient 3- Ask the image whether it needs anything from you.
>
> Ingredient 4- Does anything more need to happen? (Optional) Is there a way you can deepen your relationship with this heart image? Perhaps it would like you to merge with it? Ask it.
>
> Ingredient 5- Thank your heart image for coming. Say good-bye in a way that feels right for both of you.

6. Make the transition to the outer, physical world (breath-body-earth-sky).
7. Record your journey.
8. Find ways to integrate your journey, to bring it into your daily life.

Chapter Sixteen
The Garden of the Soul

I magery can be used to allow something which is invisible to be seen. Working with the image of a garden is a beautiful example of this style of imagery.

For centuries gardens have been places where God and man intersect. Gardens are cultivated space. They are arranged and tended by man but are wholly dependent upon the miracle of invisible life within the seed, the soil in which they take root, the elements of air and weather that nurture them, and the mystery that allows life to reveal itself, unfold, and move through its cycles. Every garden is a unique expression. The garden is a combination of what it contains, where it is planted, how it is arranged, how it is nurtured and maintained, and how the garden itself interacts with and expresses vitality and life force.

This intermingling of man and nature that is known as a garden can become an image picture of that place inside you where your individual life connects with the greater mystery of life. Invoking the image of a garden can be a discreet way of looking at your soul and of checking in and connecting with this region that defies outline and definition. Once the image is clearly with you, the inner garden becomes a place where you can rest within your soul. It is more than just a special place; it is a place that is filled with the essence of who you are and suffused with the presence of God.

The usual course for planning a garden involves considering what you would like to grow (for beauty, food, or medicine), how you would like to arrange what is growing, and what elements you would like to incorporate (paths, gates, fountains, statuary, ponds, bells, benches, etc.).   Ambient factors such as color and design, borders, or plantings that encourage other life forms are among the possibilities that may be incorporated. When planning a garden, you individualize it by including the aspects that are important or pleasing to you. You also consider the area where the garden will be; its climate, the soil conditions, the amount of available light. Conditions of reality mix with inner promptings as form is given in what you plant, how you plant it, what you include, and where you plant your garden.

This is an exercise of viewing the soul through the imagery of a garden. Looking inward allows the garden to reveal itself to you. You are not planning it. You are looking to see what is there. The inner essence reveals itself through the inner picture, which gives itself to you through imagery. Instead of creating garden space that reflects the qualities that you love, you are letting the soul reveal itself in its own way through the metaphor of garden. In this garden you can get an idea of what is going on within you on this level. You can rest there and breathe the fragrance of your soul.

Doing Soul Garden Imagery

This type of imagery is frequently without dialogue. It is an asking and a looking. The more formal pattern of the five essential ingredients in the "recipe" is often absent because of the absence of dialogue. You become a visitor in your own garden. As with other types of imagery, the preliminary steps are important. Protect the space. Pray. Quiet your mind. Relax your body. Invite the image to come forth.

I like to treat the imagery garden as I would a real garden, taking time to wander and observe, exploring the different elements that are present there, taking in the scents and the colors, the different spaces of the garden... in other words, taking a tour! Let this tour take as long as you'd like. Allow yourself enough time and space to get an idea of size, of diversity of life present there, and of areas that draw your particular attention. Notice what is growing, the colors around you, and the sounds that come to you. Are you aware of seasonal cycles (bud, blossom, seed and fruit)? Does anything about the soil or the air draw you? Do some areas need tending? Are other life forms present?

Be aware of how you feel. Find a spot that feels right for resting, a spot that invites you to relax. Breathe the air of your garden. Does this place seem to send a message to you?

Spend as much time as you'd like in your inner garden, allowing room for anything that needs to happen there. When you are ready to leave, express your gratitude in a way that seems appropriate. Begin to let your awareness come back into the physical world as you return your awareness to your breathing and to the ground beneath you. Take your time. When you are fully present and engaged with your physical senses in the outer world, take some time to record the details of your imagery or bring awareness of your visit into the physical world in some other way.

If, in your inner travels, you have found that the soul needs some tending, you may find it helpful to engage in activities that feed your soul. Some examples of soul nourishing activities include silence, solitude, simplicity, laughter, rituals that touch places of mystery, encounters with creation, journaling, free time, prayer, and heartfelt communion with others.

Give your garden the food that it needs and return to it as often as you'd like. This inner garden is always there, offering you its pure air and matchless energy.

Some Garden Stories

When I first did this type of garden imagery, I was amazed at what I saw in my inner garden. The garden stretched out to cover ground as far as the eye could see. All kinds of things were growing, in all seasons of growth. I specifically remember sunflowers, wild violets, okra, gentian, corn, roses, sweet potatoes, honeysuckle, and grasses of all types. I remember thinking that this garden held enough food and beauty to feed the masses. I was truly humbled by the magnificence of what I saw. The vision of my inner garden is a very real part of the energy behind the writing of this book. I wanted to share the beauty and strength of this work, and my garden imagery reassured me of plentitude and showed me that I had enough to share.

I offer this soul garden imagery to groups and am always surprised and delighted by the individuality of the imagery and by how it resonates with the person to whom it comes. I share here the stories of several group members who visited their soul gardens.

*

Celia is 65. She does not garden and does not feel any particular resonance with gardening, although she enjoys gardens. She is a nurse and a harpist. Here is her imagery:

"When I enter my garden, I find a huge area with fields of wild poppies, and a stream with a waterfall. Purple mountains rise majestically in the distance. Everything is very green. The air is bright and clear. As I sit on some stones in the garden, an egret lights beside me, and it seems to say, "Look at you! You can flap your wings and fly!"

Celia described the experience as a time of "oneness and attunement." She returned from the imagery with a sense of freedom, solitude, and quietness.

*

Colleen is 45. She was raised in a strict Pennsylvania Dutch family and works as an elementary school teacher. Her garden imagery follows.

"I see a little rectangular garden by a garden shed. Brown Eyed Susans and Queen Anne's Lace grow here. This part of the garden is wild and tangled, and rabbits love it here. A long, green snake makes his home here, and little white butterflies fly through the air. All of this is accompanied by the sound of cicadas. Very manicured grass surrounds this wild area. Around the perimeter of the green grass stand huge hardwood trees with bare branches. Birds are singing. As I rest here, a large white owl flies in and lands on the garden shed."

Colleen described the imagery as portraying her "wild at heart" quality, which was surrounded by the manicured grass that portrayed the way she had been raised. The trees seemed to her to depict the way she showed herself to the world. She left the imagery sensing that changes in this place were the terrain of God and that she had little mortal control of what would manifest there.

*

Joan is a gifted body worker in her mid forties. Her skills and reputation as a healer grow daily. Here is her inner garden imagery:

"This is a formal garden. I see a stunning peacock

107

walking through a very proper lawn. A huge mansion is in front of me with hedges on both sides. On the right side, I see a hedge maze which I can discern from an aerial view. I see a long swimming pool in which I am swimming! Elegantly dressed people are drinking wine.

"On the left, I see a rusty old gate. Everything seems dead and gray, and the mansion looks haunted. I ask, "why am I here?" I see myself in white shoes and white gloves. I touch the ground and sunflowers burst into life where my hand touches the earth. The house transforms into a magnificent white mansion. I see my father walk out of the mansion. He comes and sits down with me. I don't want to leave this place."

Joan describes her feeling following the imagery as one of profound contentment. Her father had died five years prior to this imagery. They had no dialogue but sat together in each others presence during the imagery. The garden of Joan's soul offered this gift to her, through her imagery. The imagery of hands that brought things to life seemed appropriate and profound in light of Joan's healing profession and the restorative ways in which she uses her hands on others as part of her work.

Doing Soul Garden Imagery

1. Protect the space. Pray.
2. Quiet your mind. Relax your body. (earth-air-breath-body)
3. Invite the image of your soul garden to reveal itself to you.
4. Take a tour of your soul garden.
   -wander, observe, and take in the scents, colors, and sounds.
5. Observe your surroundings.
   - become familiar with the garden's lay-out.
   - observe size, diversity of plant life, what is growing there, and the seasonal cycle of the garden and it's contents.
   - notice any areas that may seem to need tending.
   - are other life-forms present? (You may dialogue with these other life-forms using the five essential ingredients).
6. Notice how you feel in your soul garden.
7. Find a spot to rest and "be," where you can absorb the energy of your soul garden.
8. Does this place have a message for you?
9. Does anything need to happen while you're here?
10. Does your garden need tending in any way? Can this happen now?
11. Express gratitude to your garden and say good-bye in a way that feels right and good to you.
12. Take your time transitioning into the outer world (breath-body- earth-sky).
13. Record your soul garden memories.
14. Re-visit often. Notice changes, and what stays the same. Put reminders of your inner garden in your outer world.

ADDRESSING CONCERNS

Chapter Seventeen
Working With Life Issues and Questions

A s humans, we are frequently faced with decision making. Counsel is sought in many different ways as we attempt to make "right" decisions. Generally, council seeking involves outward inquiry using various resources which can include the surveying or questioning of friends, acquaintances, and authorities. Sometimes a professional counselor is sought. Many people turn to inner approaches such as prayer and contemplation in the face of decision making. In gathering the information needed to make or support a decision, individual styles vary. Some people will rely more heavily on one approach than another. For people who rely heavily on feeling, a decision often becomes clear only after they have chosen one way or the other, and then can "feel" that this was or was not the decision they wanted to make. For those who rely most on thinking, common sense and practicality take the major role in decision making. For those who are sense-based, a gut-sense will likely steer their decisions. Most of us use a combination of these qualities to assist us in making decisions. Imagery offers a different way of knowing. An exploration using imagery is a sound way to involve your inner knowing in the dynamic process of making life decisions and working with specific issues and questions.

I love the phrase "gather your forces." It suggests bringing all of your helpers together and rallying around a certain question, issue, or situation. The phrase brings to mind an assembly where each voice is heard and where each member gathered can contribute from their individual expertise. The help from the inner world is not visible to the physical eye, yet it is powerful and effectual. Balancing what is gleaned from outside sources with information from within becomes the task at hand. Your deepest self has knowledge to share with you. It can do that by giving form to itself through imagery. The helpers in the inner realms are representatives or symbols of the inner knowing. When you are "gathering your forces", you can use inner work to balance and complement the knowledge and information that you acquire from the outside. This inner consultation will help to put you in harmony with your own cadence so that the decisions that you make and the way you approach problems and questions will support your true and whole self, bringing you closer to the truth of your own nature.

How to Work With Issues and Questions Using Imagery

Take some time before your journey to gather your thoughts regarding the issue of inquiry. Suppose you are involved with a decision about moving to a new town. In a sense, you want to consolidate what you already know about this move. Though not essential, paper and pencil are great helpers in this mental preparation. You can write or put on paper that which you already know, including what you have been told by others, what you have learned from resources outside yourself, pros and cons, your emotions regarding the issue in question, and factors which you know will influence your decision. This collection of outside information will help clear the way for the inner work.

I have already written about the special place and the inner friend or counselor. These are helpful tools to use when working with specific issues or questions. The special place helps to link you with your inner world and becomes the inner container where your journey unfolds. When you enlist the help of the inner friend, you have a companion for the journey, one who can become a guide if you are not sure how to proceed or if you feel stuck or scared. I like to think of the presence of prayer on both sides of the journey, the outside and the inside. Prayer influences the qualities of trust and protection in your inner work. Increased trust and protection invite an expansion of freedom as you allow the journey to unfold.

Now you are ready to journey. You have prepared the space and invited your mind and body to relax. Bring your question or inquiry to mind. Experiment with holding it lightly in your awareness, consciously opening the space for insight to come. Begin by imagining your special place. This may be a place that comes to you specifically encircling the question or inquiry with which you are working, or it may be a familiar place that has become well known in your imagery. Truly feel yourself there in that place. Become familiar there as you attune your interior senses to the inner world. When you are ready, ask that your inner friend or counselor be present with you. Invite this friend to come forth. You have held the question or inquiry, so the images that materialize in your inner imagery will be related to your inquiry, even if they do not readily appear to be. The inner friend that comes may be a familiar inner friend or perhaps a being whom you have not yet met. Take some time to get to know the place and the friend who have come to you. Use the five essential ingredients. When you feel you have established a foothold in the place, ask your inner friend to stay with you while you look at the question or issue of inquiry.

If you are comfortable in the inner world, these first steps (special place, inner friend) may be bypassed as you proceed to call forth the image. Your approach to the journey becomes a matter of choice and style. Using the example of a decision which involves moving to a new town, you might now call for an image that would represent the prospective move. You can shape your inquiry to satisfy what you need or want to know.

Ask the question or issue to take the form of an image. Be patient as an image reveals itself. Remember that this issue or question may take a form that makes sense to your thinking mind, or it may take a form that is totally surprising and strange to you. What comes may be a single image or an unfolding adventure. Observe the image, take part in the adventure. Get to know it. Again, let respect, hospitality, and the five essential ingredients be your guidelines. What do you notice? Does this image bring a message? What does it have to show you or tell you? What does it need? What needs to happen? Stay engaged. Ask questions. Respond to the imagery that is coming to you. Direct your questions to the imagery that arises. Tell the imagery how you are feeling. Your inner friend is there for you if you need help. Participate in the conversation from the deepest levels of your being. Be very honest. If you begin to feel lost or overwhelmed, share this feeling with your inner friend. Honesty will change the imagery in ways that you will find to be helpful.

Remember that the world of imagery speaks its own language. The information and substance that you glean from this world will probably not come to you in a clear and succinct one-line answer (in this world, though, anything is possible!). Observe what comes. If you feel you need clarity, ask for it. See what happens. Use the sequential steps of the five essential ingredients as you allow the imagery to develop. When you experience recognition of completion, ask the imagery if it is time to say good-bye. Thank the imagery and the characters that have come to you. Thank the place. Say good-bye in a way that feels right to you.

Review your journey and record it. What impressions are strong for you as you review and record? Journal your impressions. Underline or make note of any words from your journey that seem particularly meaningful. Find external ways to interact with the images from your interior so that integration can take place. Allow the inner world to influence the outer world.

Some Imagery Stories about Life Issues and Questions

I'd like to use an example that illustrates imagery regarding the question about moving to a new town. Katie is in her thirties and married to a lawyer. Her husband has been offered a position with a law firm in a large city where an old friend of his is a partner. They currently live in a small town, where their children attend school and where Katie grew up. Katie's husband has told her that he would enjoy the challenge of the new position, but he is happy in his current practice and enjoys their rural life. He has asked her for her input, and has told her he would be willing to go or to stay. Katie turns to imagery to explore the advice of her innermost self. Here is her journey:

"I am in my special place, a grove of trees. The trees are birches and their leaves whisper in the wind. I feel calm here, and the weight of this decision seems somehow lighter. I feel myself resting here. (Katie takes some time at this point to just rest in her special place, taking in all the peace she is experiencing.)

My inner helper (Katie's word for her inner friend) is here. Her name is Patches. She is a white cat with black patches. She circles all around me while she purrs. She is graceful and gentle, and wears a small bell around her neck. I greet her, and ask her if she would accompany me as I look at the possibility of moving. She curls into my lap and opens her eyes wide, affirming her willingness.

"I call for an image that would represent the decision about moving. What I see is a mouse running into a hole. It wants me to follow it. As I follow it into its hole, I see a cozy living room and a little table, as though I am in a child's story book. A braided rug covers the floor, and pictures hang from the walls. I remember a story from my childhood, about a city mouse and a country mouse. The story comes back to me. It was about the wonders of the city, and the great fun the

mouse had visiting his city cousin, but it ended with the mouse longing for the open space and good air of the country. I tell the story to the mouse as I sit in a little chair in his home. I feel a bit "closed in" down here in mouse's house, like I need some air. I become aware of Patches now, and I hear her bell. Her paw swoops down and scoops us up, the mouse and me. She puts us down in the city. We are in a park. People and activity surround us. The mouse runs down a hole, right there in the park. I follow. This little home has locks on the doors and windows. As I look at the walls, I see some beautiful paintings that I recognize, and I remember the art museum that would be so close-by if we lived in the city. Again, I feel the air choking me, but this time it smells stale with a hint of exhaust. I ask mouse what he needs and he says one word, "air." When I ask what needs to happen, I know that I, too, need to breathe fresh air. I find myself back in the grove of birches with Patches on my lap. As the lessons become clear to me, I think of mouse, Patches, and the beautiful birch grove. I send them a thank you and a grateful good-bye."

Katie understood the message she received from her imagery. City living would be too restrictive for her nature, but she would enjoy all the city had to offer. She also knew that she wasn't really serving herself in her present situation. The stuffiness of mouse's hole in the country was overriding the coziness of it. Katie saw this as a picture of her present situation. Although no firm decision about moving was made based on this imagery, she felt she had learned things of which she had not previously been aware. She knew that wherever she lived, she needed fresh air and new experiences. Katie made a commitment to herself to expand her horizons, for herself and her children "no matter where we live", and felt new peace with that decision.

*

Brigit is 54. She works as a secondary school teacher while maintaining a part-time body work practice as a cranio-sacral therapist. She comes to her imagery session wanting to explore the "blocks" that keep her from fulfilling her greater purpose. She wants to look at her own resistance. Underlying her inquiry are the broad questions, "How can I be of service?" and, "What am I supposed to be doing with my life?" She holds these questions in her mind as she begins her inner journey.

"The memory of a sunlit room comes to me. This was a cottage where my parents took my brother and me as children. I have the sense of my brother napping and the perfect golden sunlight that filled the room. I remember talking with my mother as we lay on the bed. It was wonderful. I feel a sense of love, of belonging to family, of the mother-daughter relationship, quietness, the light, and the aroma of summer. Most memorable are golden light and the depth of the feelings.

When I ask my resistance (to fulfilling my greater purpose) to come to me as an image, I see a little girl dressed in yellow. She is stomping her feet in an expression of defiance. She does not want to be disciplined. I am aware that she does not want to figure out what she is supposed to do with her life, nor does she want to do what she is supposed to do. She sees these as one and the same. I am also aware that she is an aspect of me. I can feel the place inside me where I am tired of working hard and don't want to explore what I'm supposed to do with my life.

As I allow this little girl to stomp and "have her fit", she transforms into a quiet and centered young woman who really looks at me. She is accepting, but seems to be urging me to be more mature about this question.

Then, as this young woman looks at me, I become aware of actual blocks in the palms of my hands. These are square wooden blocks, and I find myself wondering if they are "sticky" and if they can be removed. I am able to remove these blocks, to peel them off of my hands like they were held there with velcro. As I handle these blocks, I am aware of the feeling of tingling in my palms that often comes when I am working on a client's body. I have not felt this sensation in a while, and this has concerned me because when I feel it, I feel "connected."

The quiet young woman is with me now. She helps me to see the fears that are underneath these blocks.

I see the fear of not doing things well enough.

I see the fear of getting into situations that I don't know how to handle.

The young woman helps me to see that I can keep these blocks stacked in the corner of my treatment room. I see that I can choose to remove these blocks from my hands. I can take these off now and still be okay. I do this. I can see them stacked in the corner. I know what they are and why they are there."

After Brigit's imagery session, she said she felt it soothing to know that the blocks she had been experiencing were not a weakness. She was able to look at the blocks as something that came as a form of protection rather than a weakness. She also felt a new acceptance and understanding regarding her feelings of resistance. After this imagery journey, she shared some observances about how this imagery influenced her work with clients on the table. She spoke about her first session with a client following this imagery. "I was aware of the blocks sitting in the corner. I chose to think about leaving them there. I felt a lot of warmth and tingling in my hands during the session, like in the "old days." My client seemed more relaxed than usual and more responsive in areas that are usually 'blocked!' (hmmm!)"

Doing Imagery around Life Issues and Questions

1. Protect the space. Pray.
2. Quiet your mind. Relax your body (earth-air-breath-body).
3. Bring your inquiry or question to mind along with the facts you have already collected about this issue. Hold all of this in your awareness.
4. (Optional) Go to your special place. Invite your inner friend to be present with you while you look at this issue. Greet and thank your friend, and ask whether there is something you need to be shown or told regarding your inquiry. Ask your inner friend to be with you while you look at the issue in question.
5. Invite an image to come forth that will represent the issue in question.
6. Begin to dialogue with the image, using the five essential ingredients.

    Ingredient 1: Greet the image. Thank it for coming.

    Ingredient 2: Ask the image if it has a message for you, something to show you or tell you.

    Ingredient 3: Ask the image if it needs something from you.

    Ingredient 4: Ask whether anything more needs to happen.

    Ingredient 5: Thank the image or images that have come. Say "good-bye" in a way that feels right to you.
7. Take time to transition fully into the outer world (breath-body-earth-sky).

8. Record your journey.
9. Combine what you have learned from your inner world with the information you have gathered about the issue in question. Find ways to remember what your imagery has shown you. Bring the wisdom of your inner journey into your outer life.

Chapter Eighteen
Healing and the Body

The human body is truly a universe. Intricate systems work separately and together, exchanging and renewing, circulating and stimulating, repairing and repressing. Individual cells do their individual jobs, nutrients are distributed, and electrical impulses are meted out in rhythms that synchronize all else that is happening. Whole systems cooperate with other whole systems. Endless activity occurs within our bodies, all the time.

Outwardly, the human smiles and cries, walks and runs, sleeps, communes, takes nourishment, loves, learns, and lives. On either end of all human activities are conception and birth, then death. On either end of these activities is mystery. The human body is an expression of all of these attributes. When one system is in danger, other systems within the body respond. The universe of the body responds.

Imagery can help you to gather your energy and use the infinite wisdom accessible in the inner realms to assist in the healing process. Imagery is valuable as a way of making sure that an essential inner component of the disease or disorder with which you are dealing is not neglected. The practice of looking within and the discoveries that can result combine with whatever healing is being sought and offered from the outer world. Inner work completes the work of healers and physicians, medicines and therapies, programs and procedures. The universe of the body seeks balance, and health is its natural, balanced state. Imagery activates or awakens your awareness of the inner world, and because of this, practicing imagery can lead you into healing because the activated inner world will move toward healing, balance, and wholeness.

Imagery can be utilized in many different ways to assist in healing. In this chapter I'll address the use of imagery for healing, working with healing images, listening to and dialoguing with your body, talking with and giving direction to your body, writing a letter to your body, and emergency imagery to use in times of stress.

Using Imagery for Healing

The Healing Imagery Journey

I like to work with healing imagery in three phases. Sometimes all three phases are used. At other times, only one or two are used. Sometimes, they all blend together. I will describe all three.

The first phase is <u>going to the healing place</u>. The second is <u>calling for the inner healer(s) to come and be with you</u>. The third is <u>going to the part of the body that is in question</u>, noticing how it presents itself to you, imagining what it would look like if it were whole and healthy, and then tracking the movement from one state to the other.

For healing imagery to occur, you go to the place where you can access all the inner help that you need. That place is inside you. How do you proceed?

Follow the preliminary steps of protecting the space, praying, quieting the mind, and relaxing the body. (Chapter 3) Hold your inquiry for healing lightly in your mind. Invite a place for healing to reveal itself to you, to come forth. This is also the place where you will later meet with the inner healer. Perhaps this is a place that you recognize. Perhaps it is a place you have never seen before. Either is fine. Remember that this place is being revealed to you by the infinite wisdom within you. Trust it. You have aligned your imaginative abilities with your greatest good through prayer and preparation, so now you must take the leap of trust, and have faith in the power that enables you to imagine and be guided to the images you need to see.

Bring yourself into full presence in this healing place by asking the sensory questions: "What do I notice around me?", "What are the colors here?", "What time of day or night is it?", "Are there sounds?", "Are there smells?" Do I sense textures?" And then, "Where is it that I most want to be in this place?" Let yourself be in the spot that feels just right to you. You may take a while to find it. That's okay. Notice how you feel. Notice whether you are aware of any healing energies that are present in this place. Be aware of them. Sometimes the place itself offers healing gifts. If you have the sense that this is a ripe place for healing, ask, "What needs to happen here?"

Continuing into the second phase of healing imagery, call out into this place and invite the inner healer to come forth. Know that this healer can take any form, and that more than one healer may possibly show up. Greet them all. If this is too confusing for you, you can ask just one to step forward. From here, proceed with the simple steps of inquiry. Thank them for coming. Ask, "Do you have a message for me?", "Is there something you need?", and "What needs to happen?" Allow a conversation to emerge. Speak to the inner healer of your fears, your feelings, and your honest response to what you are being shown and told. If you are willing, engage in the activities suggested by the inner healer. As you prepare for the third phase, determine the willingness of the inner healer to be with you as you look at the part of your body in question.

With the inner healer(s) present (if they are willing), ask the body part in question to show itself to you in your imagery. You may have a good idea of exactly what is happening in your body because it has been explained to you by your health-care provider. In your inner vision, you may receive an actual image of the body part in question. However, the image that presents itself may be purely metaphorical. Notice the image very carefully. Take time to observe details. Perhaps the image itself will speak to you. Perhaps your inner healer will have things to say to you about what you are seeing. Perhaps you will get impressions from the image. Notice everything. Be a part of what is happening.

Now, ask the image what it would look like if it were whole and healthy. Notice what happens as it moves from one state to the other. Ask it what needs to happen for it to be whole and healthy. Ask, "How might this happen?" Invite the inner healer to participate in any way that is helpful. Be very present with what is happening. When you have a sense of the imagery being complete, be certain to thank the images that have come to you. Ask whether you could receive the gift of a healing image that you could hold in your mind and body. Remember this image. Say "Good-bye" to the figures and places of the inner realms. Breathe into your body. Allow your senses to return to the physical world. Record your journey. Work with the images that have come.

Working with Healing Images

Working with healing is an ongoing process. Doing imagery and then forgetting all about it will not be as effective as continuing to work with it. How do you work with your imagery? Return to it regularly, at least every day, ideally several times a day. You need not engage in the whole imagery process again. Just return to the key images, the ones that have stood out for you in the journey. Perhaps you can use some words from the journey as affirmations. The picture of movement from the image of the problem toward an image of wholeness is a powerful tool with which to work on a daily basis. Find a realistic way to follow suggestions that may have been given in the imagery. If you are comfortable sharing the imagery with your health-care provider, do so. Hopefully, he or she will respect the images and the work you have done. More and more, this kind of inner work is honored by physicians and their assistants. Do not allow a dismissal of your inner work by another to diminish the value you place in it. They simply may not be able to understand what you have learned. Recognize and value the work that has come from your depths, from your innermost self where you connect with the Great Knowing. It is work that is wholly worthy of your attention.

Listening To Your Body

Engaging in Dialogue

You can learn to listen to your body. Your body knows things. It knows where you have stored pain and pleasure. It has been your earthly home since you were born. Your body speaks to you in different ways, such as sensation, well-being, and disease. Imagery is one way that your body can from a bridge with your mind and spirit to communicate with you in a clear way.

In my work as a yoga teacher, I am always encouraging my students to listen to their bodies. This listening is more like listening in their bodies, because you cannot hear what your body is really communicating unless you are present and attentive within it. If your body is desperate for your attention, you may find yourself forced to pay attention by occurrences such as disease, injury, or pain. A preferable pathway is to give loving listening and attention to your body before it has to get your attention in a more extreme way.

I often ask students to form an intention before a yoga class begins. A beautiful intention is simply to listen to your body. The intention of listening puts a different spin on everything that occurs during the class, because whatever occurs within this container of intention can become listening.

You do not have to be in a yoga class to participate in inner listening. Form the intention to listen. Become receptive. Relax into your body. Notice what happens. Respond to what you notice as you would in conversation. This is dialoguing with your body.

Listening to your body can take place during any activity where you can turn your attention inward, such as walking, running, or sitting. You do not need to have a specific reason to listen deeply to your body, but there are many occasions where this can be helpful. Here are some examples:

Dialogue with an organ before its scheduled removal can help to prepare you on a deep level for the giving up or easy release of that organ. Thank it for all it has done for you and let it know what is going to happen and what you expect of it. Ask it whether it has something to tell you or show you before it is removed. Speak with it as you would an image that has come to you.

Perhaps you've had a certain problem for a long time. Talk to your body. Talk to your headaches, talk to your nervousness. Talk to your symptoms, especially if you have done everything else and don't know what else to do. Form the intention to listen, and then listen. Be receptive. When you are listening, respond to what you are sensing as though you are in conversation with a friend. Perhaps you will "hear" in images. Use the recipe to work with them. Perhaps you will "hear" in sensations or feelings, thoughts or memories, insights or gut senses. Again, use the recipe to respond, asking the key questions: "Do you have a message for me?" "Is there something you need?", "What needs to happen?" All of these are ways that your body can communicate with you. Respond, and then allow your body to respond. This is inner conversation, or dialogue with your body.

Talking With Your Body.....Giving Direction

Communication with your body is an integral part of healing. Your body is receptive to your voice. You can comfort yourself in times of stress and make suggestions that will encourage movement toward healing. When these suggestions are grounded in the inner work of imagery, they become even more effective because they have originated from within. Sometimes, however, something needs to happen and your body needs to be asked to respond. An example would be cessation of bleeding following an injury. You are not helpless and separate from your body. You are intimately part of each other. You can ask your body to stop bleeding. Relax as much as you are able to. Sometimes this means talking to your self from a calm center even though things are outwardly chaotic. Tell your body what needs to happen. The more details you can provide the better. Your words might sound like, "Blood vessels, you need to constrict so this bleeding stops." Picture that constriction happening. Let your body know what you'd like it to do. Slow your breathing and make it even and regular. This will aid in relaxation, even in times of great upheaval. *The more relaxed and authoritative you are, the more receptive your body is to suggestion.*

Treat your body like a wise friend; let it know what is going to happen and what you would like from it. Sprinkle gratitude into your conversation. Use affirmations to help change old ideas that don't align with healing.

You can use some direct tools in imagery to support what is happening with your body and what you would like to have happen with your body. Sometimes these helpful tools come from your own imagery, but sometimes they come from the wisdom of others and can be incorporated into your own healing. You may hear or read some words that resonate deeply with you. (ex: "In the presence of fear, I relax, knowing my Lord is with me.") These words can be incorporated into your "talk" with your body.

Great strides have been made in the area of healing and

imagery and I have included sources for learning and study in the bibliography. Imagery tapes that cover a range of specific situations and illnesses are available. You may find the entire tape helpful, or you may listen to it and choose some statements that feel "right" for your situation and needs. Tell your body what is going to happen and how you would like it to respond. Remember to include words of gratitude.

I will give an example from my own life. A surgeon was explaining a certain procedure to me. As required, he was also sharing with me some things that might "go wrong." In this situation he was explaining how my bladder would be lifted during the course of some upcoming surgery, and he told me that sometimes it takes a while for the bladder to begin working again after surgery because it is "shocked." As I thought about his words and applied my knowledge of imagery and the body to this situation, I decided to talk to my body... to let it know exactly what was going to happen (so it wouldn't be "shocked!"). I listened to the words of Drs. Martin Rossman and David Bressler, with whom I had studied (see bibliography). They offered specific suggestions that would be beneficial during surgery. I coupled these suggestions with how I would like my body to respond. To communicate this information with my body, I decided to write a letter.

Writing a Letter to Your Body

If you have the blessing of time to prepare for something that is going to happen with your body, you can choose to write a letter.

Some factors that I included in the letter that I wrote to my body are common to most surgeries, so I will include them here because they may be helpful to you or to someone you know.

For example, it is generally helpful for blood to be kept away from the operative site during surgery, returning after surgery is complete. This redirecting of blood flow allows for decreased blood loss during surgery and a clearer view of the operative area. Muscles and organs should stay relaxed. The bowels and digestive system need to resume normal function when surgery is complete, thus avoiding ileus (failure of the natural movement of the intestines). The immune system needs to keep the area free of infection. The lungs need to clean themselves after surgery, removing any accumulated wastes and filling the body and with life-renewing breath.

Certain specifics that are unique to what is being done can be addressed with every surgery. In the pre-stated instance involving my bladder, I told my bladder it would be lifted. I asked it to please continue working after the surgery (and it listened!).

Another example might involve the removal of a tumor. You could ask the tumor to free itself easily into the surgeon's hands and visualize that release happening. The same holds true for an organ that will be removed. Ask it to release easily. Write your hopes. Write your expectations. Communicate honestly and clearly. Include your hopes and affirm your health and the things that really matter to you. Then read what you have written. Read to your body as though you were reading to a friend.

Emergency Imagery in Times of Stress

Remember that special-place imagery can be a good tool to use when you are nervous and frightened for your body. Common examples of body related nervousness can be found in a dentist's chair or a hospital procedure room. Imagery can help your body to relax. The calming effects of imagery are enhanced by controlled or conscious deep breathing, slow and full. The creation of a regular, slow, and deep breathing pattern is a very powerful helper in itself during times of stress, and its helpfulness increases when it is coupled with imagery. No matter where you are when you need to relax, even though you are feeling tense, begin by slowing and deepening your breath, and then imagine yourself in a place where you love to be. Use your imagery skills to stay present and you will find your body responding by staying relaxed. This will be helpful not only for you, but also for those working with you.

Some Imagery Stories of Healing and the Body

This journey belongs to Sue. She is 51 and has had a major recurrence of breast cancer, with the cancer spreading into other tissues and systems. She has had to stop teaching and is on a vigorous chemotherapy regimen that is debilitating. I see her in her beautiful home, and we sit on the porch in the sun and talk. Sue is candid. We discuss possibilities. She speaks of her mother and sister, who have died of this disease. Here is part of her imagery journey:

"As I breathe in, I sense green; as I breathe out, I let go of a sick yellow color. In my mind's eye I see the trails behind our property. I see chairs there. The view is familiar and good, full of good memories. I come to the place where I pause when I walk. I sit in an Adirondack-style chair. I watch for birds. Sometimes the crows announce the presence of Red Tailed Hawks. I see an old maple tree. The top half is dead. The bottom half is full of green leaves. I think how the top half is a good place for birds. In the distance I see trails for walking and skiing. I feel peaceful, expectant, and calm as I invite my inner healer to be present. What I see are the chickadees! A downpour of rain arrives, and they are out there playing in the rain! Their message to me is this: They are so small and seem so insignificant. They are powerful for me. They know joy in all kinds of horrendous situations. They play in blizzards! They show me light. They tell me to be aware of the joy that is in me. They tell me to be aware of joy itself. They do want me to be well. I keep asking why. What should I do if I can't be well? They tell me to play in the blizzard.

"I see an Indian princess now. She is very brave and

very wise. She has such strength in her. Her strength goes beyond anything in the physical world. I think she's always with me. I just don't notice. I think I need to notice. She comes to me as an image to use when I need to call up my strength.

"Hawk is here too, telling me that sometimes I just have to get out of my body and escape. I can do this by soaring, like Hawk, higher and higher in circular flying. Hawk tells me flying is especially good over fresh water. I do this when I have my chemotherapy.... Hawk and Indian Princess tell me to use them as often as I can to lighten the load. I see my skin as pink and healthy. Good fluid runs through my cells, nourishing them. They tell me to hold this image and work with it. As I thank them, they already know I am grateful. I am grateful for their example and their steadfastness."

Postscript: Sue had a brief period of increased strength, and then became much weaker. She died a little over a year after doing this imagery. Even as she became weaker, her attitude was amazing. I often saw her "playing" with her friends, going to the movies, laughing, and enjoying life. Even though I know things were not easy, her final year of life was good, and she told me that her imagery was strongly with her, helping her.

Growth and healing can occur even if they are not physically evident in a full recovery. As a nurse, I have observed this many times. As humans, we love the stories of miraculous recoveries. And yet, and importantly, healing and growth are possible even when physical recovery is not. I include Sue's striking imagery here to illustrate this point, and to honor her beautiful spirit.

*

Pat is in her early sixties. She is a pianist and has a performance scheduled for mid-June. On a March afternoon, she tripped on a city sidewalk (while going to see the film, "The Pianist!"!) and injured her shoulder. She endured terrible pain during the film, and sought medical care immediately afterward. Pat was told she had a broken shoulder bone, a broken upper arm, a torn rotator cuff, and tendon and muscular trauma. She saw a specialist who treated her with immobilization, ice, and pain medication. This management was to be followed by surgery at a later date as the broken bones of the upper arm were out of alignment, and the rotator cuff was torn and twisted. She decided to use imagery to assist in her healing. This imagery occurred 4 days after her injury:

"I am sitting in a small, round room, similar to a gazebo. All around me are open arches and curtains blowing in the breeze. I see no windows. Everything is cool and white.

"I invite my inner healer to join me here. I see a wise, bearded man. He is tall and thin. He comes behind me and lays his hand on my shoulder. His hand is huge. He speaks with me about doing everything I am told to do. He tells me that my doctor knows what I need to do, and reminds me to be compliant with the suggestions of my entire medical team. He says he will be there with his hand upon me. I imagine his giant hand on my injured arm and shoulder, sucking out the pain and hurt while slowly healing my injury. He tells me to spend time visualizing this occurring. I thank him as we part and return to physical awareness with the sense of his hand still upon me."

Pat did as she was told by her medical team and by her inner healer. When she returned for her last check-up, she expected surgery to be scheduled. X-rays showed that both pieces of the upper arm bone had returned to proper alignment, the shoulder bone had returned to its proper position, and the rotator cuff was no longer twisted! Surgery was canceled. The doctor told Pat he had never seen anything like this before. Here are Pat's words:

"It remains a bit of a mystery to me; was it the imagery and visualization, my positive attitude, my desire to meet my goal of presenting a concert in mid-June, my friends praying for me and sending well-wishes? How does one separate mind-body-spirit? I don't believe we can, and I believe it was all of the above. When my body was hurting, I believe all of these allies were here to help me over the rough bumps!!!"

*

The following journey is my own. This imagery was part of the surgical preparation that I did prior to the fore-mentioned operative repair procedure. A childbirth related weakness in my pelvic floor had gradually worsened necessitating this fairly major operation.

"As I go to the healing place, I am aware of a stream and sand. The sun is shining, and a blanket lies on the sand. I call for my inner healer. I see an Indian man with long, dark hair and an eagle mask. He has white wings. He is lean and strong, with dark eyes. I also see Elephant (an animal I have known since I first did imagery). A horse is here, too. Horse is dark with a black mane and tail. They tell me they are a team, a medicine team. They invite me to lie on the blanket. The Indian takes my head and cups his hands around the base of my skull. Elephant is on my right, very happy. The horse is on my left. I am aware of an angel at my feet. The angel is not fully visible, but I am very aware of its presence. The angel and the Indian are working together, supporting the deep rhythms of my

body. I feel myself release into their holding. They tell me they will do this before, during, and after the surgery.

"I ask them to be with me as I look into my body, into my pelvis. I see the image of a mortar and pestle (the bowl and wand used traditionally for grinding herbs). It is made of stone. I sense a weakness at the very bottom of the bowl or mortar, as if it were crumbling. I ask to see the image that would represent wholeness and healing, and I see the same vessel with a re-plastering of masonry that has rebuilt the wall. I ask my body what it wants to tell me. I hear, "Someone needs to do the work." I get the sense of a blessing on the upcoming surgery. Hands bless my body and bless the medical team that will do the work. I feel the blessing move forward to the time of the surgery. I sense my helpers around me, the Indian, Horse, Elephant, and Angel. I am asked to hold the image of the medical personnel being blessed. All four directions where my helpers stand are being blessed. Then I hear the words... "repair and artistry." I see an image of the Sistine Chapel, the beauty of that repaired chapel with the restored painting on the ceiling. I know everything will be all right. I am told to hold the image of this part of my body as a chapel. My four helpers will be with me during the surgery, surrounding me and protecting me, seeing that all goes well."

When I did this imagery, I had not met my surgeon. When I did meet him, I looked at his hands. They looked like an artist's hands. Months after a successful procedure, I lay on his examining table, and he looked at the barely visible scar from the incision he had made. His nurse stood by his side. She leaned over and said to me, "He's really an artist you know."

Doing a Healing Imagery Journey

1. Protect the space. Pray.
2. Quiet your mind. Relax your body (earth-air-breath-body).
3. Imagine yourself in a healing place, a special place where you love to be.
    - Ask, "does anything need to happen here?"
4. Invite your inner healer to come forth, and dialogue using the five essential ingredients. (Greet and thank your inner healer for coming. Ask, "Do you have a message for me?" "Is there anything you need?" "What needs to happen?")
5. Ask your inner healer if he or she would accompany you as you look at your body or the part of your body in question.
6. Call out inside and ask the part of your body where you are experiencing dis-ease to reveal itself to you as an image.
7. Carefully observe the image that comes as a representative of your illness or problem.
8. Begin dialogue with the image. Request the participation of your inner healer.
    - Ask, "Do you have a message for me?" "Is there anything you need?" "What needs to happen?"
9. Now, ask the image to show you what it would look and feel like if it were whole and healthy. Request the inner healer's presence and participation as this image reveals itself to you.
    - Ask this image of wholeness if it would offer a gift in the form of a healing image with which you can work.

- Ask, "Do you have a message for me?" "Is there anything you need?" What needs to happen?"

10. Thank the images that have come to you. Say good-bye.
11. Take your time returning to the physical world (breath-body-earth- sky).
12. Record your journey.
13. Create ways to integrate your journey and work with the healing images you have been given (see Chapter 8).

Doing Listening and Dialogue with Your Body

1. Form an intention to really listen to your body. Combine this, in your own way, with prayer.
2. Relax your body. Quiet your mind.
3. Engage in any activity where your attention can turn inward (such as yoga, walking, jogging, or sitting).
4. Allow yourself to become receptive. Pay attention to whatever happens, be it thought, sensation, images, or memories.
5. Respond honestly to whatever you are seeing, feeling, thinking or sensing. Converse with your body as you would converse with a trusted friend.
6. Remember these elements: "Do you have a message for me?" "Is there anything you need?" and "What needs to happen?"
7. Finish your session with gratitude toward your body.
8. (optional) Record any thoughts you may have about this time of listening.
9. Think of ways you can incorporate what you have learned into your life, and do this!

Talking With Your Body by Giving Direction

1. Relax. Quiet your mind. Breathe deeply and slowly.
2. Turn your attention inward.
3. Tell your body what needs to happen. Remember this: The more authoritative and relaxed you are, the more receptive your body is to suggestion.
4. Let your body know what is happening, and what you would like.
5. Use gratitude and affirmation in your conversation.
6. Visualize whatever you are asking. See it happening.
7. Talk to your body as though it were a friend.

Writing a Letter to Your Body

1. Begin your letter as though you were writing to a dear friend. Speak to your body with loving words (ex: dear, beautiful, beloved, cherished).
2. Tell your body what is going to be happening, to the extent that you know this.
3. Let your body know what you need it to do and what you expect of it. Be clear.
4. If you so desire, write your innermost hopes, including what you wish for your body.
5. Read the letter you have written to your body. Read as though you were reading the letter to a dear friend. Read it often.

Doing Emergency Imagery in Times of Stress

1. Breathe in a slow and regular rhythm. Deepen your breathing, allowing your abdomen to expand as you inhale, and emptying completely as you exhale.
2. Let your mind focus on the rhythm and evenness of your breathing.
3. Imagine yourself in your special place.
    - Involve all of your inner senses.
    - Look at everything around you. Observe colors.
    - Listen to the sounds of your special place.
    - Notice smells, textures, temperature, and time of day.
    - Allow yourself to be wherever you would most like to be in this place.
    -Breathe here.
    -Repeat any words or focus on any images that give you comfort.

Chapter Nineteen

Exploring Relationship through Imagery

Relationship pervades life. You are in relation with all things, in many different styles and ways. Some relationships are assumed and given very little thought until they are somehow interrupted. Other relationships become the focus of thought and seep into all other parts of your life. Relationship with others is usually intricately involved in your own happiness and also in your sorrow. Inspiration to expand into new and different areas of life is often catalyzed by associations with others.

On the dark side, relationship can become obsessive, crossing the invisible boundary of soundness and moving into precarious territories such as fixation. An uncomfortable relationship can bear you down and steal energy from you. As great as this power is, so also is the power of relationship to enliven and renew. Relationship can open your very pores to new awareness and depths of wonder. We need others physically, emotionally, and intellectually. We need others to help us understand the world, each other, and ourselves.

The topic of relationship has been a major focus of human inquiry throughout history. Oracles, psychics, and those acclaimed for their wisdom have been called upon throughout the ages to provide insight into relationships of love. The posed query has remained basically unchanged. "Help me understand my relationship with my sister, my brother, my daughter, my son, my lover, my boss, my teacher, my counselor, my boyfriend, my girlfriend, my husband, my wife." This is very likely a request with which we can all identify. As humans, we want to grasp and understand what is happening as our lives intersect in a major way with that of another.

Inquiry into the relationship between two people is very mysterious ground, and imagery can be helpful. Understand that the "letting go" that is required as you enter your imagery is even more pronounced when exploring relationship. Leaving your wishes and dreams "at the border" as you enter the world of imagery with relationship can be difficult. Still, it can be done, and the insights provided by this exploration can be profound, helpful, and insightful.

If you are separated from one whom you love, either by distance or by differences, the mid-way place between the two of you can be fertile ground for exploration, communication, healing, and togetherness.

The Place Between

The midway place between two people is potent. Recognition of this between-place where spirit is strong and present can affect the exchange that occurs. When you consider the metaphor of human beings as little worlds, one world can have a profound effect upon the other. In seeking to understand relationship, some aspects will always remain a mystery. In a family, all have grown together through proximity and blood, influencing and circling one another sometimes for years and sometimes since birth. You usually have some experience of collision with each other and not getting along, but also some experience of the kinship and love that secures the galaxy formed by the members of the family. Familiarity exists; formalities are dropped. Quite often, a decline in respectful behavior and a show of unfavorable conduct can manifest when you are around those with whom you are closest. Perhaps this scenario occurs because you are so familiar with each other. Respect becomes the challenge and the healing balm of any relationship.

144

Outside of family, you'll find an even greater sense of "otherness" in relationships, such as differences in cultural and social codes of behavior. The understanding of unspoken rules may differ greatly from one person to another and one social structure to another. Human guidelines of respect are the codes that can help ease you into places that are mysterious and unfamiliar. While raising my children, I have tried to teach them to act with respect and courtesy, thinking that these skills will help them to make their way through whatever life might bring. These same codes of respect and courtesy are the guidelines that accompany you into imagery that explores relationship with another. (Actually, these guidelines are present in all imagery but are accentuated when inquiring into relationship.)

A certain respect is called for when approaching another. This fact is true in the visible world and is also true in the world of imagery. Say you are seeking to better understand your relationship with a friend. The imagery around that relationship needs to honor the boundaries of your separate worlds. The place where the two of you come together is the invisible place between the two of you, the place midway. Both of you have equal footing in this place. It is the place where your two worlds touch. No breech of boundary occurs when you explore this place. You belong there as does your friend. It is a place that can bring form to the mystery of intersecting with each other.

I remember reading about a practice of the late Pope, John Paul II. I have not been able to rediscover this article and name its source, so I share this as story although it may very well be fact. The article described how the pope prepared for meetings with foreign dignitaries by sending his angels out to meet the angels of the other so the way would be prepared by these holy emissaries. This idea struck me as a beautiful a way to approach another; from the place that already exists between you before you have even met. I began to approach my students in this way when I was teaching. I would light a candle for my students and connect the place between us with thoughts of our angels and a prayer that I would give my best and be open to what needed to happen. I will never know for certain whether this practice was helpful to them, but I know it was helpful to me.

Entry into this potent between place where the presence of spirit is strong can affect the exchange that occurs in any relationship. The power of this place is not confined to relationships of friendship. For example, imagine bringing awareness to the place between you and the check-out clerk at the grocery store, or between you and the waitress who serves you in a restaurant. Imagining Spirit's presence between yourself and any other being changes and deepens the tone of the encounter. Try it! It is an interesting and enlightening practice.

Doing the Imagery

Make preparations for your journey. You may want to include a request directed toward your thinking mind to "let go" as you relax and pray, entering the space of imagery. Bring to mind and heart the relationship you are seeking to explore. Imagine the two of you and invite the place *between* you to come to form, to reveal itself to you. I find this place usually shows itself as a landscape, but be open to possibility. It may present itself differently to you.

Open your inner senses and be fully present in the place that is revealed. What are the characteristics of this place? What are the sounds, the colors, the feelings of the place? Do you see yourself there? What are you doing, and where are you? Do you see the other person there? This may or may not be so. Try not to force anything or anyone to be there. Just notice what is already there. In this scene, is there a spot where you would like to be? Give yourself time for exploration, noticing what is around you. When you are ready, settle into a spot that feels right. Ask the place, "What needs to happen?" Be open to what unfolds. Perhaps images with which you would like to dialogue will be present. Perhaps you are content to just be there in a spirit of openness and exploration. If you do have specific questions, you can voice them and open yourself to response.

Remember that this place you are visiting may have a somewhat different language from your own imagery because it touches the world of another. This "touching" also means that a subtle exchange is possible. Be aware of this. You may want to leave a prayer or a blessing there for the other person, a signal of your attention and care. If you feel unsure or uncertain, you can invite a guide or helper to be there with you. When you feel this imagery coming to a point of closing, acknowledge and thank what has come to you. Talk to the landscape, thanking it for revealing itself. Say "good-bye" in a way that seems right and honors your intuition.

In this kind of imagery, much is unsaid. The journey is like a respectful visit to a place where no invasion of another's privacy occurs but where you can be "together" in a symbolic type of energy sharing. If you'd like to record your journey, and work with it, feel free to do this. Many things are happening when you intersect with the world of another. If you so choose, you can enjoy this journey without the requirement of formal integration work. Integration is happening through the model of this respectful visit to the place between one another. Return as often as you wish. You may find it interesting to note changes in the place and changes in your way of being there. An old bit of wisdom declares you can never enter the same river twice. With this same understanding, no two visits to the place between you and another can ever be the same.

Some Imagery Stories from the Place Between

Loretta is in her 50's. Her grown son Josh is in the army reserves and his unit has shipped out to Iraq. I shared the basics of visiting the "place between" with Loretta. This is her imagery:

"I close my eyes and think of Josh, especially his eyes. I remember those eyes from the first time they looked out at me. I think of him now, a grown man. I am still able to see the sweet child inside his grown man's body. I ask to visit the place between us. I immediately see a tree. It looks like a fruit tree, and it is in full bursting bloom. Soft blossoms are falling. This tree is the only vegetation that I see. The land is vast and stark. In the distance are mountains. I go to the tree and stand with my back against the trunk. I sense Josh there, on the other side of the tree. His back is also against the tree. We face in opposite directions with the tree strong between us. I send him the love from my heart. I feel that it circles the tree in wide rings, touching Josh and spreading out beyond us both.

I slide my back down the trunk until I am sitting on the ground, my knees bent and my feet flat on the earth. I pray for Josh's safety. Somehow, my prayers cannot stop there. I feel the rings of them spreading out from this place. I pray for all the soldiers. I pray for their families. I pray for the Iraqi people, especially the children. I pray for the Iraqi soldiers and their families. I pray for the land itself, so devastated by war, yet able to grow this amazing tree.

"When I ask what needs to happen, I get the urge to leave a note here. I take pen and paper from my shirt pocket. The paper is blue. I write my prayer. I write of my love for Josh. I write down a prayer of protection that I learned many years ago. This is my prayer: 'The light of God surrounds you. The love of God enfolds you. The power of God protects you. The presence of God watches over you. Wherever you are, God is.'

"As I stand up, I am aware of the scent of the dry air and how it mingles with the smell of the blossoms. I kiss the blue paper before I hang the note. I reach around the tree and pierce the note with a small branch, attaching it to his side of the tree. I know I will come back here often."

Tears fell as Loretta described this place between herself and her son. She spoke of the comfort she felt in being able to "be" with him from an inner place, even though he was so far away. She said that she now writes letters in both worlds, those which she writes in her living room to mail to Iraq and those which she writes in her mind to hang on Josh's side of the fruit tree.

*

Jana and Ray have a loving but stormy marriage. Jana has felt a barrier that she would like to "see". She longs to feel close again. She describes their partnership as herself being fire and him being water. "He puts out my fire and I boil his water." Here is Jana's journey to the place between them.

"I am in a farmer's field. The earth is freshly turned. Some dogs are here and they are really happy. I think these are dogs we used to have when we were first married, although they look different in this place. I am on the crest of a hill. The woods border the boundaries of the field. I smell the dark earth that has just been plowed. No noise of traffic enters the space of this field. The dogs flank me. I feel good and warm here. I would like to leave Ray a sign of peace, a little altar of stones, left as a sign to him that I am on his side and that I want peace. I don't want war.

"I begin to pile stones. The dogs remind me of loyalty. I remember how they used to buffer the bad feelings between us and how our love of them shone through our bad times and diffused bad feelings. I have a turtle trinket that I lay on the stone altar. I prick myself and leave a drop of my blood there

too. I want him to know how deeply I feel about us. I write "Jana and Ray" with the blood. The dogs leave their paw prints beside my writing. I say a little prayer.

"I ask then if a message from him would reveal itself. My eyes go to a big and scraggly tree that I hadn't seen. It is huge and old, yet beautiful in its scraggliness. It seems to say that its heart is good, that it is still alive."

Jana felt pensive and open after her imagery. She sensed a message from the tree, asking her not to compare her trials to those of Ray. She felt a renewed commitment to him. She also sensed a lot of healing in the presence of the dogs, even though they had died years before. "They are a bridge between us, there to bring out the love."

*

My father is having some surgery. I am physically far away from the place where this is going to happen. I look at the clock and see that the time of his operation is nearing. I want to be with him in prayer and support while he undergoes anesthesia and surgery. I bring him to heart and mind and close my eyes to "visit" the place between us.

"Several landscapes filter through my mind but do not stay. I become aware of a long stone table/bench. The atmosphere is that of a park or a public place, and the season is spring, as the trees are in bloom. As I look around, I see a marble building with pillars. I recognize the Lincoln Memorial in Washington DC. I am vaguely aware of the Washington Monument. I experience strains of memory, of visiting the capital city of my country with my father as a child and again as an adult. I lie on the sun-warmed table/bench and become strongly aware of my

father. He was a teacher of history and government for many years, and this place seems just right as the place between us.

"I am aware of his kindness and his sense of justice, his humor and outgoing friendliness. I am grateful that he is my father, and I whisper this gratitude to the place. I am aware of the vulnerability of anesthesia, and I pray for him. I pray that he may be safe and held during the surgery; that the doctors, nurses, and attendants may be skilled and careful; that his body may respond with health, and that his suffering be little as possible. Mostly I give thanks for his life as it has been, as it is, and as it shall be.

"I get off the bench/table and imagine it being prepared for him as he is readied for surgery. I take sage and light it, passing the smoke over the bench-like table in a Native American ritual of smudging, preparing sacred space. I imagine him being held by his guides and angels during the procedure, though I know not who they are. I am deeply aware of my love for him."

I feel at peace after this pre-operative "visit" to the place between us. I have the feeling that I have done what I can do.

Doing Relationship Imagery in the Place Between

1. Prepare for the imagery. Ask your thinking mind to let go.
2. Protect the space. Pray.
3. Relax your body. Quiet your mind (earth-air-breath-body).
4. Bring to mind and heart the relationship you are going to explore. Gently focus on the thought of both of you.
5. Invite the place between you to take form in your imagery.
6. Become receptive. Observe everything in your imagery.
    - Notice the characteristics and qualities of the place between.
    - Notice sounds, colors, smells, temperature, and light.
    - Do you see yourself here? Where are you?
    - Find the exact spot where you want to be, and be there.
7. Ask, "What needs to happen here?"
    - (Optional) Dialogue with another in this scene may be appropriate if someone else is there and this feels right.
    - Allow yourself to be fully present and attentive in this place, engaging in whatever needs to happen.
8. If you have come with questions, you can pose them in this place between. Your questions do not have to be directed toward anyone, just spoken to the place as it has come to you.

9. Is there something you would like to leave here for the other person? Is there something they have left here for you?

10. Thank the place and any others that have come to you there. Say Good-bye in a way that feels right to you.

11. Take your time coming back to the physical world (breath-body-earth-sky).

12. You may record your journey, or just review it as you would a visit with another. Know that you can return. Follow through with anything you have agreed to in the journey.

Open-ended Imagery

Chapter Twenty
Wide Open Imagery

I mmersion in imagery does not require a specific inquiry or predetermined focus in order to be helpful and effective. Your inner world is always available and able to determine the needed direction independently. Interestingly, in open-ended imagery the inner world often offers something of which you weren't even aware. Regular engagement with wide open imagery keeps the conversation between the outer and inner worlds alive. Regular inner check-in can help you to stay fresh and in tune with the deeper levels of perception and awareness within you.

In this type of imagery, the strong container provided by special place and inner friend are bypassed (unless the imagery itself takes you to them). As you become quiet in mind and body, you call for whoever or whatever is most needed now, in the present time. Control is relinquished to the wisdom within you as you invite the images to come. From that point, the formula of the five essential ingredients is there to see you through your imagery.

For those with a passion for imagery and for those who work with imagery and maintain a regular practice of their own, this type of imagery is very common. A great trust is implied as you enter the inner realms saying, "What do you have to show me?" And "What is important for me now?" Receptivity and listening come into even finer tuning as the unknown unfolds within you. Sometimes you have no clue where the imagery is going, and patience, trust, and attention are required as the imagery finds its way to fullness.

Wide open imagery takes you to the images that your inner

nature knows you need. Imagery comes from your soul. I try to remember this when engaging in open-ended imagery. I am being taken someplace where I need to be, and the emphasis is being chosen by the deepest part of me. You will notice pointedness as you work with this imagery. The deeper self has a keen aim and will take you to the stories and images that will restore, strengthen, and tend to you.

Stories from the Land of Wide Open Imagery

Frederica is 50 and a masterful body worker. She has moved from the east coast to the Rocky Mountains. She is a seasoned "journeyer" and is familiar with imagery. Before her imagery session she speaks of feeling a block regarding weight loss, concerns with her marriage, and a muddiness that she cannot seem to wade through. She has addressed these issues through traditional and alternative health care avenues and turns now to imagery for insight. She enters the imagery wide open, calling for whoever or whatever needs to come. Here is her journey.

"I close my eyes and see the mountain that I look at every day. My mind goes straight to the mountain's core, and I am aware of how it presses into the Earth. I feel its presence near me as a blessing. I think about the conflict that is sometimes present in my marriage, the conflict regarding the extravagance of living here. The mountain dismisses this as not important.

"I am aware of the big metamorphic core of this mountain and the solidity of its being. I sense my own core. Just because it has been a bit shaky does not mean it has not been there. I have the sense of the mountain sharing its obsidian core

with me, making it available through the Earth on which I live. I feel the strength of the mountain in my own core, as though it has come into me.

"The mountain gets a big smile on its face. It tells me that everybody has their own relationship with him. He can handle all of it. My relationship with him is very unique and only for the two of us.

"I see the image of a round, salty cracker and am reminded of my own association with carbohydrates and how I look to them to fill the hungers in me. I hear a message that tells me to increase my intake of minerals and to get out and touch the Earth.

"The mountain is my lover but not in a way I've ever known before. I see the image of a beautiful beaded turquoise belt with white and orange beads and fringe. It is my gift from the mountain. I feel resistance. I put it on anyway, around my waist, my least favorite part of myself. It is very beautiful. It feels so strange to be gifted and adorned. My hands lift up toward the mountain. I see a piece of red coral in my hand. I want to give the mountain something from the sea. He accepts.

"My head is spinning 110 miles an hour. I tell the mountain. He gives me another gift, a band of white beads. It goes around the top of my head. I feel crowned. I can give him <u>anything</u>, and what I will get back is a gift and a blessing. My body feels stunned.

"I am told to find something white and keep it nearby, a white vessel. I am told to put a few beads in it, blue, orange, and white. I am told to put more beads in it everyday as a representation of the gifts that are coming to me..."

Frederica was not certain of the meaning of her journey, but she trusted and accepted it as what she needed. The element of Earth was coming into her, and she was allowing it to do so. A deep, wise part of her had accessed these images and she would let them integrate with her.

Frederica had worked with the inner world enough to know that she had a choice following this imagery. She could keep the imagery alive and weave it through her waking hours or let it sleep and seep away from her consciousness. She could honor it with remembrance and by doing what it asked of her, by revisiting it often. She could also dismiss it. Her choice would determine whether the imagery would continue to help her move forward with its teachings.

A few weeks after this imagery, I received some photographs and a letter from Frederica. She had fashioned a bowl of white clay, and every day she would drop a few beads into it as she spoke her gratitude and prayers and brought her awareness to the message of the mountain. I share here an excerpt from her letter:

"Maybe this imagery fits into the issue that has become identified for me over the past several years -- that of my belief that my gifts are all for others and not for me. I will use myself to exhaustion to keep others going-- and I am learning to be present for others from strength and grounding rather than from a survival mode which is a default mode and is very destructive to my body and soul. My loving gifts, creative gifts, wisdom gifts, are present for others and not used for myself.

"So, given that setup inside, my ability to receive is about as developed as my ability to relate to a mountain inside me. It's not on the map. I can do it, but I have no program that relates to it, and therefore I am in an arena that requires faith and the ability to walk out into nothingness with no tools--that wonderful edge place where it is important to remember to breathe, since all rote patterning stops, like the earth holding still before breaking into bloom, and we must think about breathing, since it is all we can do there. Meanwhile, I drop beads in the bowl, and remember the mountain that speaks to me as a lover."

*

Sally is 46. She is married with children still at home. She has happiness in her career for the first time in her life. She has done imagery before for specific reasons and now wants to "check in" with her imagery. Some issues with the heart and relationship are up front for her, but she wants to trust the imagery and see what it considers "up front." Here is her journey:

"As I close my eyes, I focus on an old white goat on top of a hill. He turns toward me, his beard prominent and his eyes sparkling. I greet him and ask if he has a message for me. "Come and look", he says. I go to the place beside him, and we look down over a civilized valley. Buildings, roads, and bodies of water are all apparent. A church steeple stands higher than the other buildings, and my attention is drawn there. Just as I look at it, I hear the church bells ring. All is quiet as Goat looks at me. "What does the bell say?" asks Goat. I listen. I hear the bell ring eight times. Its sound covers the valley and reaches easily to my place on the hill. I am eight years old. I sit there with him, wearing a dress my mother has made. Somehow, I see my adult self beside this little girl who is also me.

"Goat ignores the adult me and speaks to the little girl. "What do you care about?" he asks the child. I listen while the child tells the goat that she is afraid. She tells him that she doesn't want to grow up, that she is frightened. "What are you afraid of", asks goat. "I'm afraid it will be too hard, that I won't do it right." Goat is quiet for a minute and actually strokes his beard! "Tell the lady that", he says. The little girl me turns toward the adult me and confesses her feelings of being afraid of how hard it is going to be to grow up. Goat looks at me and says nothing, but nods his head. I take the child in my arms. I look at her and see my own children. I see the child I once was. I tell her to look at me. I tell her I am happy and that God has given me great gifts that I never would have expected..

"She shows me a spot on her dress where she has spilled something. I tell her not to worry. Things get messy, and that is part of everything. I hear myself telling her that the most

beautiful things in life are usually a little bit messy. I take her hand, and I feel her warm little fingers close around mine. I give her the gift of my blessing. She says she wants to be with me still, and we look to Goat for advice. He walks between us and sits down. The little girl climbs under his front legs and comes into my lap. I assure her of my protection. I tell her she can be with me. I welcome her. We ask Goat whether anything more needs to happen. He lies down. He wants us to touch his back, which we do. "You are both so fine," he says. We look down at the civilization below. I hold the little girl who is a younger me in my lap and thank her for coming to me. I feel my heart opening to all children. I kiss her on her head and pat the goat as I say "good-bye" and "thank you" to the place that has held this imagery."

Sally was surprised by what came to her. She wondered aloud about time, as time seemed to take a different form in the imagery. She felt her own blessing extending backward into her growing up years and spoke of feeling a new vulnerability and completeness as she returned from her journey with her younger self. "I could have never guessed this was what I needed," she said. "But it was."

Doing Wide Open Imagery

1. Protect the space. Pray.
2. Quiet your mind. Relax your body (earth-air-breath-body).
3. Settle into your inner awareness. Call out, and ask whatever or whomever is most needed at this time to come forth.
4. Greet whomever or whatever comes to you. Thank them for coming.
5. Inquire, "Why have you come?" "Do you have a message for me?"
6. Allow the conversation and imagery to unfold and reveal itself.
7. Ask the images that have come if they need anything from you.
8. Ask what needs to happen.
9. Deepen your relationship with the imagery in any way that feels appropriate (merging with an image, asking questions, sharing honest feelings).
10. Before saying "good-bye", ask whether anything more needs to happen.
11. Say good-bye and offer gratitude in a way that feels right.
12. Come back into full awareness of the physical world (breath-body-earth-sky).
13. Record your journey.
14. Make note of any actions in which you are being asked to participate. Find ways to bring the journey into your real world. Follow through with anything you have said you will do.

Chapter Twenty One
When Time is of the Essence

Careful preparation can help to build a strong container in which imagery can happen for you, but the luxury of time is not always practical or possible. Sometimes the need to gather your strength and assemble your best self arises quickly, without prior notice. Sometimes the pace of a given period in your life just does not offer loads of time in which to buffer and balance the noise of the world with practices of turning inward. And yet, to ignore the voice of the deep self is a sure mistake in many ways. Staying in connection with the deeper rhythms of your soul is the true habit that will see you through the busyness, chaos, and the times when you are called upon to grow, to be more than you think you are. We are all asked to "rise to the occasion" in small and large ways every day. Inner imagery is a wonderful helpmate in this endeavor.

A minute or two is all that is truly necessary to turn off the chatter of the mind and to ask for an image to come forward as a helper. I use the formula of breath-earth-image. I'm certain other ways exist, and perhaps you will find your own way of reaching the inner place of imagery in a short amount of time. I will share this formula (breath-earth-image) that I have found helpful and that has worked for many others. The key is to find your own centerpoint and to call forth the image from that place. Many different practices teach many different ways to enter deeply into the stillness of being. This is the quick trip!

Calling For the Quick Image

If you are able to closet yourself away from the world for just a moment, you will find that privacy is helpful, although not absolutely necessary. Visit the rest room, any private area, or just close the door. If even this is undoable, inconspicuously turn away from others and close your eyes. If you can't do this, just turn your attention inward for a moment, even with eyes open.

Engage in the formula of breath-earth-image by beginning with breath. Pay attention to a full cycle of breath; inhale and exhale. A prayer can accompany the breath. This only takes a few seconds. Give this cycle of breath your full and complete attention. Let your breathing be deep and even. Then, give attention to your feet on the floor. This will help to bring awareness to your body and the earth beneath you. Feel the place where your feet meet the ground. Imagine the whole Earth beneath you. Again, this takes only seconds. Now it is time to call for an image. Do this, and accept what comes. Knowing why a certain image has come or even understanding how it will help you are not important. Just take a minute to receive the image and its details and energy. Thank the image and return to the setting or situation as you breathe this image into you, letting it become a part of you.

This type of imagery usually precludes dialogue because it lacks the time for it. You simply let the image become a part of you, and you are subtly different as a result. The energy of the image is now part of you on a conscious level. The image can aptly affect your carriage, your voice, your body language, and your demeanor. It can give you strength, courage, perspective, and a host of other qualities that are tailored specifically to the situation in which you find yourself.

Author and poet David Whyte speaks eloquently of the image coming forward in his book, "The Heart Aroused" published by Currency Doubleday. Here are his words:

"This summoning of internal imagery may seem like the description of amazing oracular powers, but it is really the simple process of uncovering something our deeper psyche already knows. The deep psyche, or soul, left to find its way, will offer up or recognize in the outer world the images germane to its place on the path of life. That's it, the soul seems to say. That's how it looks from here...

"...the important thing is not to overinterpret the image... We place too much burden on it if we are too quick to say it must mean this or it must mean that. The main point is to live with the image... and let it work its magic on us."

In the same work, David Whyte gives the following example of imagery at play in the corporate setting:

"The image will not only give an indication of strategy, but also tell us what way we should *be* as we navigate the situation. It may be the image... of a bull asking us to dig our heels in and lock horns... we can hold our image of locking horns in the mind's eye even as we are speaking with our antagonist. It is extraordinary how much of the power carried by the image itself will be present in our voice."

Some Examples of Quick Imagery

Rita is afraid of flying. She has worked with this fear in many ways, but when the time comes to board the plane, she needs some help to walk through the boarding corridor. Here is how she describes the imagery that she did at this critical moment:

"I take a deep breath and let my feet feel the good ground beneath me. I ask for an image. What I see is a little bear, a Koala, hanging onto a tree with his paws wrapped around it.

167

He is high up in the air but calmly holding on.

"*I walk right onto that plane and sit down. I hold the comforting image like a child who holds a stuffed animal! As I look out the window of the plane, I can't believe my eyes. I can see a Qantas jet taxiing down a runway to my right. It is decorated with the symbols of Australia, the home of the Koala! This confirms to me that my journey in the sky will be fine. I take it as a sign! Although I am still on edge, I feel something in me settle down.*"

Rita is still afraid of flying, but she does not let this keep her on the ground! She now has a tiny stuffed koala that she carries with her during flights for comfort and good luck. The little stuffed bear reminds her of the message she received from her own deep self, from a place that helped her to override her fears.

*

The first day of school has arrived for my daughters, who are entering third and sixth grade. The summer has been full and busy, and I have not given the time I had hoped to give to discussions regarding feelings about the coming school year. While getting hurriedly ready for school on this first morning, I decide to guide the girls into some quick imagery as we walk to the bus stop. Here are their quick imagery stories:

I ask Lyssie (6th grade) to close her eyes and call for an image that will help her with 6th grade. *She sees an elephant, who says, "Remember, you are Lyssie. You are special. Life will go on."*.... I ask her to breathe in the words and the image. She does.

Then I turn to Marina (3rd grade). I ask her to call for an image that will help her through 3rd grade. *She sees a little panda.*

It tells her "Whatever happens, everything will be OK. Mrs. Summers isn't going to mind." She smiles as she takes the image in on her breath. I could almost hear it land in her body!

These images stayed with my daughters throughout the school year. I found pictures of their animals and wrote the animal's messages on postcards that I gave them to help them integrate their imagery. I know the images saw them through that school year in ways that were totally unique to each of them. I did not fully understand either message, but that was OK, because they did. I often wonder whether the messages didn't deflect some fears that both children were consciously unaware of and therefore unable to articulate. This practice of calling for an animal to help them through the year has continued in our family, and is now a first day of school ritual.

*

Cindy is a photographer and a busy mom in her late thirties. She is in the middle of a very busy month of dealing with an intensely full schedule and describes herself as feeling "very pressed." Following a brief relaxation based on breath and earth connection, she calls for an image. Here is what she sees:

"I see a great bird. It is flying; actually it is gliding. I hear the word "accept."

I talked with Cindy a week later. She said she was enjoying her bird image. She pictured it "gracefully swooping around, gliding on the breeze, surveying the territory below...while deciding what to pounce on and what to pass up!" In relation to her busy schedule, she described herself as feeling "in command of my environment .... and at ease."

*

Kate is a musician in her early sixties. She is feeling some angst about "having to deal with the IRS and a few other things equally as pleasant." She gratefully embraced the idea of calling for a helpful image. Using the breath, earth, image formula, she closed her eyes and called for an image. This is what she experienced:

"I see a water buffalo with big, huge horns. The animal itself is totally serene and very strong. I know from my travels that the buffalo with the large horns are especially revered."

When I next saw Kate, she told me that she had brought the water buffalo in front of her several times during that busy period of her life. "I imagined walking to these stressful events with great purpose and strength, slowly and gracefully, revered and breathing."

Doing Quick Imagery

1. Find a place where you can take a private moment for yourself. In lieu of this, turn away from others for a moment. Close your eyes if you are able to do this inconspicuously.
2. Use the formula of breath-earth-image.
   - Take a full conscious breath, paying attention as you inhale and exhale deeply and fully.
   - Bring your attention to your feet against the ground. Feel the support of the whole earth beneath you.
   - Call out for a helpful image from within.
3. Receive the image that comes to you. Take in the details and energy of the image. Breathe this image into you, letting it become a part of you.
4. Thank the image.
5. Take a transition breath as your attention moves back to the situation at hand. The energy of the image will be with you.

Part Four

Some Final Considerations

Chapter Twenty Two
The Presence or Absence of a Guide

For many people, maintaining the focus and attention required to stay with their imagery as it unfolds on the inner screen can be tedious and difficult. This difficulty is common, and can often be overcome through practice and patient discipline. A trained imagery guide is not always available in the moment that imagery is necessary, so knowing how to guide yourself is a wonderful skill. The intention of this book is to give you the simple tools that will allow you to self-guide.

If you have the opportunity to journey with a guide, you will see that the imagery process becomes even fuller, with more room for depth and focus. I will discuss both types of inner journey, imagery done with a guide and also without.

Doing Imagery with a Guide

Good imagery guides will hold a sacred space for you. They will keep you connected with the imagery that is happening for you. Focus will be easier to maintain with the help of a guide. Your inner being can then immerse itself in what is happening because the guide will be there, metaphorically holding the door open and watching over you.

Many counselors and therapists have the skills to guide you. I have included several resources in the back of the book, organizations that can direct you to trained practitioners who specifically work with imagery. You may hear this type of imagery called "interactive imagerysm," "deep imagery," "animal imagery," "personal imagery," and "The Personal Totem Pole Process™."

If you have trouble finding a guide in your area, some guides are willing to work over the phone. Find one who will keep you linked with your own imagery, one who will not interject opinions or direct the course of the imagery in interfering ways. Trust is essential between you and your guide. You have both the privilege and responsibility to talk with your guide about how they will work with you.

If you enlist the help of a guide, take some time to prepare yourself before you meet with him or her. Do not assume that your guide will give you time to prepare the space, to pray, to help you connect with your deeper rhythms. You can do this beforehand. Even if a time lapse exists between when you do your individual preparation and when your guide leads you through the imagery, early preparation will be better than plunging in unprepared. Self-care continues to be important after the journey. Perhaps your guide will discuss ways to integrate your journey when it is over, but this cannot be assumed. Integration work (see Chapter 8) which you can do on your own will strengthen and enrich the bridge you have built between the inner and outer worlds. In many ways you are still caring for yourself even in the presence of a guide. Make sure the essential questions are asked. If they are not, you can ask them yourself in your imagery journey.

Finding a trusted practitioner and being able to release into his or her trusted care while you journey is a remarkable experience. I hope this will be possible for you if this is what you desire. However, it is always wise to hold your own council, making certain what is happening is what needs to happen. In so many arenas this holds true. In the field of medicine, you find a doctor you can trust, but you also weigh what you are told with what you already know and have come to hold as truth. This also holds true in the fields of religion and education, to name only a few. In diverse areas, human beings are learning to discriminate objectively rather than to blindly trust authority. This is certainly true as you choose a guide to help you look inside and learn from your inner teachers.

If a trained guide is not available to you and you have a trusted friend who is familiar with "the recipe" and the guidelines outlined in this book, you can try working with him or her, perhaps exchanging imagery sessions. If you do this, try to stay objective. Refrain from voicing your own opinions and steering the direction of outcome when you are guiding someone else. Remember that the imagery itself is in you, that it is available to you no matter where you are, and that it can be entered into with or without a human guide. (One of my daughters does imagery on her own with her heart animal guiding her!)

Doing Imagery on Your Own

Sometimes at night, when sleep will not come, I sense that sleep is being prevented by something in the inner world that wants my attention. I turn my awareness inward then and invite an image to come forth. You can do this, too. You'll find that when you have a clear understanding of the simple steps (the "recipe), you possess a container that can hold whatever needs to happen.

When you are doing your own imagery without a guide, have a clear idea about the steps you will follow. These steps then become your guide. Once you become comfortable and have experience with the imagery process, the steps will become second nature. In the beginning, however, be aware of the reason you are doing the imagery and the steps you will take (having a copy of the "recipe" in front of you will cue the steps for you).

Try not to be discouraged if you find your mind wandering. Just come back to the imagery. At first, you may need to bring yourself back to it several times. The process itself will help to bring you to a clearer focus. Discipline presents an interesting contrast here, for while you are disciplining yourself to stay with the inner imagery, the imagery itself is totally free to go where it will. The thinking, chattering mind may pull you away from the imagery. Just tell yourself that you will return to the imagery. This is natural, so you can set aside any feelings of failure or inability that may result. Return as often as you wander, and finish when you have a sense of completion. If distraction is a problem for you, keep in mind the factors that may be helpful in self-guiding, such as writing your imagery as it happens and using drumbeat or music as a backdrop (see Chapter 9).

Remember that the more you work with your imagery, the easier it will be to journey inward. This is something that is in you and part of you. You are not teaching yourself something new, but waking a part of you that is already there, that may have been sleeping. Stick with it. As you become more and more comfortable with your inner world and learn to trust it, you will enrich your being with an active and full inner life.

Chapter Twenty Three
Imagery with Children

C hildren love to do imagery. Imagery is natural and fun for them. The whole world comes around them in a playful and creative way as their lively imaginations help them to take part in life. A child can find joy in imaginative interaction with almost anything. Work and play are inseparable as the child learns about life through all that is available to the imaginative mind. The natural faculty of imagination is so strong in children that it seeks an outlet in play wherever it can, helping them to make sense of the world and find their place in it.

A child's imagination is strong enough that it seeks an outlet, sometimes going awry when not directed in helpful and nurturing ways. An example of this occurred in the rural Pennsylvania town where I live. A fifth grade boy came to school with a gym bag full of guns and ammunition. He was dressed in full camouflage. This tragic scenario ended with a self-inflicted gun shot and suicide. The plan that emerged as his friends were interviewed had an even larger scope and had been thankfully averted. It was later revealed that this boy had an obsession with a certain video game that focused on tactics and weaponry, camouflage, and espionage. His fertile imagination had latched onto this and when he brought it out into the world with him, tragedy ensued.

Imagery emerges as a means in which a child's natural abilities to attune with the imagination can be nurtured and supported. This healthy relationship with imagination can bring richness and blessing into the lives of children as their inner worlds help to balance the strong influence of media and orchestrated play that have become so prevalent in the lives of children. Children can then come to their years of development with a valuable tool for understanding who they are. They can carry in their knowing a strong sense of the inner resource that is always available to them through imagery and their own inner faculties.

Like many other skills that a child learns at a young age, imagery is best taught through doing. Part of the beauty of doing imagery with children is the strong sense of authentic attention that children receive from the adults helping them. They are being metaphorically held in a very comprehensive way while doing imagery with the help of an adult. They are being accepted. They are being heard, and someone is listening to them. Along with these outer experiences, they are exploring their own world through their own inner faculties and learning to learn from their own reservoirs of wisdom... and there are animals there! And trees and trolls a whole world of creative adventure!

Imagery is also a way to get to know the child with whom you are working. All children are unique. The inner world of a child will reveal what is really going on for them. Sometimes children have difficulty knowing why they are feeling out of sorts, much less articulating that feeling. Their imagery will help them to know more of themselves. It will also help you to know more of them, so you can help and support them appropriately.

Helping a Child to Do Imagery

In general, children do not need the same preliminary work that adults need when preparing to do imagery. They are already ready! If they do need some help with preparation, usually some reassurance that you will stay with them is enough. Explain what you will be doing and assure them that you are going to be with them while they look inside themselves. If they are tense, you can suggest they relax their bodies, letting their bodies be like jello or wet noodles! If they still need help, you can lead them through their bodies, encouraging them to relax each area. You may find it helpful to take a few moments to center yourself before you help them, to quiet your mind and connect with breath and body, to pray. As you sit with a child before doing imagery, you can ask if he or she would like to close their eyes. This is not essential. Often, children do not need to close their eyes to do imagery. Invite them to listen to their own breathing as they relax. This might make them feel silly, (I'm not sure why, but this is my frequent experience!) but it will not detract from their experience. Just proceed. Visiting a special place and meeting with a heart friend are good starting places from which to introduce a child to imagery.

Have them imagine themselves in a safe and special place where they love to be. Have them tell you where they are. Ask them questions, "What are the colors around you?", "What are the sounds of this place?", "Is it day or night?", "Is it warm or cool?", and "Where are you in this place?" Suggest that they relax in this safe place as they get ready to call for a heart friend.

Ask them to imagine their heart. They can put heir hands there as they call for a friend to come, a friend that knows them and loves them. Let them know that it can be a plant, an animal, a person, or anything! Ask them to tell you what it is when they "see" it. When they tell you, have them say "hello" to it and thank it for coming. Remember that your job is to keep them connected to their imagery and not to interject your own opinions (not always easy!).

Have them ask their new friend whether it has something to show them or tell them. Use the simple formula of the five essential ingredients. Ask the child to tell you what they are being shown or told. If things are not going well, you can have them ask a helper to come from within their imagery. Use the basic elements of the recipe to help connect them with whomever or whatever is there. Suggest that they ask their new friend whether it needs anything. If it's okay with the child, have them give it what it needs. Have them ask their heart friend what needs to happen and encourage them to allow this if they are willing. A nice way of closing involves asking whether the heart friend would like to become an even better friend. Have the child acknowledge what is said and, if willing, participate in the friendship-deepening activity. When the time comes to say good-bye, suggest that the good-bye can happen in any way that feels right to the child.

When working with children, spend a little time with them when the imagery is over. Sometimes they will want to talk about it, and sometimes not. This is a good time to let them know that you love and care about them. Help them to find ways to remember their imagery, perhaps letting them draw or getting a book out of the library that relates to the imagery. They could make up a song or a dance that takes them back to their imagery. Don't force it, but support it. There are so many ways to integrate the inner journey with the outer world (See Chapter 8, "Integrate the Journey" for examples). Encourage and support them in finding their own creative ways to bring the imagery's messages into their lives.

Different Ways and Reasons to Do Imagery with Children

You don't need a special reason to introduce children to imagery. The activity itself is usually so natural and fun for children that they enjoy it anytime. Special place and heart friend imagery are always appropriate, and familiarity with this imagery during times of calm will foster ease and familiarity when doing imagery during times of stress. The times that I find imagery to be especially helpful are during an illness or injury, and at times when children are mentally or emotionally upset or distraught and in need of support and advice.

In times of physical sickness or injury, I have children visit the part of their body that is sick or injured. I may have them visit a special place first, as this will help to establish them in their imagery, but this is not always necessary. At any point in the imagery, you can ask them to invite a healing helper to be present. I then have them ask the sick or injured part of themselves to come to them as an image or picture. This is a way of discovering what pictures they hold in their body/mind of what is going on inside them. The images that come are frequently a collection of what has been explained and understood combined with the child's own deep body knowledge. Have the child ask the injured or sick part what it needs. Perhaps they will actually be able to give the image what it needs. You may also glean some helpful information that can be used in treatment. I almost always have children ask what that part of the body would look like if it were strong and healthy, if everything inside were healed and working well. Sometimes, a movement occurs from the picture of dis-ease toward the picture of health. You can ask them what needs to happen to move from one scene to the other, what needs to happen to move toward healing. The healing helper often facilitates this. I have successfully used this basic pattern of imagery in many different circumstances. It provides a strong container which holds the child's imagery and facilitates healing.

If children are in a panic, they may need you to begin the imagery for them. This helps them to settle down. Begin by describing a place that you know they love. Ask them to pretend they are there. Ask them to pretend there are "helpers" there too, healing their bodies (One of my daughters has a whole troop of fairies and trolls that live inside her and help her with whatever needs to be accomplished with her physical body). Ask them to "see" the healing happening (ex: the pain going away, the bones knitting together, etc).

The age and nature of the child will be a strong determining factor in how things proceed. Especially with emotional issues, different aspects of the imagery will take on new levels of importance. Body image is very important to most adolescents, and this aspect usually finds its way into the adolescent's imagery. As children move toward adulthood, their strengths are often emphasized in their imagery, as though their inner beings are making them aware of the unique gifts which are theirs to offer to the world.

I have used imagery with my own children since they were toddlers. It has helped me to raise them while honoring their individual natures. I have worked with adolescents in trouble, and have seen them connect with their deep selves through the images that were revealed to them as they found rest and resource within themselves. My dream is that imagery will be taught to children as the natural process that it is, that the generations yet to come will know and use the power of this gift that lies within, a gift that connects them with all that is.

Some Children's Imagery Stories

When my oldest daughter was 8 years old, I was told she required an orthodontic procedure called palate expansion. The aim of this procedure is to widen her palate (the roof of her mouth) by use of an expandable metal appliance that is securely attached to the palate. The palate is then "stretched" by expanding it with the turn of a key on a daily basis. The concept of this procedure was frightening to me and seemed archaic. I wanted to hear what her own inner knowing had to say about this. Here is her journey.

Lyssie closes her eyes. I ask her to call for an image that would represent her palate. She sees a little turtle there named

Johnny. Johnny wants to take her into his cave. As she describes the cave to me, I ask her what needs to happen. Johnny tells her she should look at the pictures on the wall. He tells her that the pictures are portraits of her ancestors. He explains to her that her palate is the same as theirs, but that they did not have the option of change. He tells her that he would like to have more room in his cave, and that for her to have more room in her mouth would be good. He asks her to visit him often. She thanks him and says "good-bye."

Lyssie visited Johnny regularly after this initial visit. She would visit him when she had discomfort in her palate and before major orthodontic appointments. The palate expander is long gone, and what could have been a very stressful time was actually quite smooth and easy, thanks to her own inner support. The situation became one in which she was a participant rather than one in which something was being done to her.

*

My younger daughter, Marina, fell on some metal bleachers while playing. The metal caught the skin just above her left eye and sliced the skin deeply. A lot of bleeding occurred, and she was very upset. Some preliminary first aid was administered, but I knew she needed stitches. While driving to the emergency room, I asked her to invite her helpers to begin the healing. I asked her to go right inside the hurt area and see them there helping. This is what she described:

"I see little animals that look like camels with sharp points on their backs. (This was followed by more tears. When the tears subsided, I had her go directly into the imagery and tell me what the little camels were doing.) "They are taking away the hurting and the black and yellow. When they are done taking away the black and yellow, everything is red. They are working very hard, and I tell them thank you."

I did not understand her imagery, but I have learned to trust the inner language, so I supported it, and helped her to stay with it. When we were in the emergency room waiting for a doctor, I had her do special place imagery. This calmed her down. The little camels were there with her in her special place, doing their color work on her injury. All the while this was happening, she was having simultaneous interactions in the outside world, talking with the doctor and nurses. She was used to doing imagery and was able to be in both places at the same time. By the time she was sutured, she was very calm, and the physician was able to do some very fine suturing on her face while she relaxed beneath his practiced hands.

*

The following story illustrates how imagery can also be helpful with common, treatable childhood illness. It can be used along with anything a health-care practitioner has suggested and prescribed. Imagery helps to move a child's perception of the treatment room from something nasty to something helpful! I will share a story from my younger daughter's imagery at age 7.

She woke up with congestion and full sinuses. She then complained all morning that something smelled bad. When we determined that the bad smell was nothing external, I decided to do some exploration through the imagery.

I ask Marina to close her eyes and tell me what the smell "looks" like. She points to her right sinus area and says it is a banana-shaped snail. The snail is not very talkative, but it does mention that it would feel good to be squirted with water. She thanks the snail and says "good-bye."

After Marina's imagery I mixed some saline (a mild salt water solution that matches the natural salt content of body fluids) and put it into a bulb syringe. She cheerfully shot this gently into her own nose (a much different scenario than if I had thought of this!). The smell and her preoccupation with it both went away following this old-fashioned treatment for nasal congestion that a 7 year old had self-prescribed!

*

The following imagery session uses a variety of techniques, such as initiating the imagery for children when they are in a panic and helping them to engage their own imagery through calling for a helper and meeting with a heart friend. My older daughter was 10 at the time of this imagery.

Lyssie was tired and seemed distracted when she went to bed. She began to hyperventilate and called out to me, "it's happening again." (I'm not sure what "it" was, but "it" took the form of a panicky asthma-type reaction that occurred several times a year when she was younger). I had learned to just stay with her when this happened, helping her to relax. The panic and its symptoms had always receded without the need for any specific medical intervention.

I knew I must help her to distance herself from her panic because I could see her anxiety escalating. Here is what transpired:

I tell Lyssie to picture herself in a cloud, up in the sky, with an umbrella to keep the sun away. (I didn't give a lot of conscious thought to this direction; I just knew she needed direction and diversion and said the first thing that came to my mind.) I ask her to imagine breath coming easily there in the lap of the cloud. She follows my guiding and tells me that she is there, in the clouds. Her breathing begins to show more ease as I ask her to describe the umbrella (engaging her in her imagery).

She describes it as being white lace with pink roses. I ask her to look down and see herself. She says that she sees herself at school, at her desk, working very hard.

I ask her to call for a helper, an inner friend. She tells me her angel is there with her. Her angel tells her not to work so hard. Lyssie responds that she can't, but her angel tells her that she can. The angel instructs her to look into her heart for a small animal that will show her what is in her heart.

I follow the angel's cue and guide Lyssie to look into her heart, where she sees Tuffy, the lion. She has met him before as her heart friend. Tuffy tells her that working hard at the same things all the time can make her feel tight and keep her away from what she really wants. He tells her that inside his heart is a magical doll. Lyssie then invites the doll to come forward. She tells me it doesn't look very magical; in fact the button of one eye is missing, and the doll's smile is fading. I have her tell these things to the doll. It is a ragdoll similar to Raggedy Ann. The doll tells her that she is a magical doll, and she has come to help bring Lyssie the things that she really wants.

The doll asks Lyssie to visit her every day for the next week. The angel confirms this and tells Lyssie to get some rest.

During the next week, Lyssie had a faithful visit with her imagery friends every night. She did this on her own, without my guiding. This imagery preceded testing for an enrichment program, something she dearly wanted. Later, her Dad unexpectedly brought a new bicycle home for her. Then she auditioned for and was accepted into a children's choir that she wanted to join. These new activities helped to broaden her outlook and balance the focus of traditional schoolwork. The lion remains a friend and guide for her to this day.

*

In my experience of working with children, I have had the privilege of helping to co-facilitate an imagery group for adolescents in trouble. Although I always encouraged the sharing of imagery experiences, these kids kept a lot to themselves and were often reluctant to share. I will never forget, though, hearing a young man named Carlos talk about meeting his heart friend. Here is his heart friend imagery:

"In my heart I meet a jaguar. It is strong and sleek. It invites me to run with him. (Carlos described feeling an amazing capacity for breath as he ran with the jaguar and experienced himself as Jaguar.) I feel an amazing power in my limbs. I come back into myself and thank Jaguar. I touch his neck with both of my hands as I say "good-bye." I want to remember this always."

Tears rolled from Carlos's eyes as he described the encounter. I will never know what Carlos's life brought him after this brief contact that I had with him, but I hope that Carlos always remembers his Jaguar heart friend and befriends the amazing strength of his own heart.

*

When I ask my children why they like imagery, they tell me it is a way of "finding things out that you didn't know about." They say it is "kind of like talking with yourself." And I would add that the self to which you talk is often much wiser than you could ever imagine. The wisdom of this inner self connects you with the great pool of knowing that surrounds you in the mystery of life. When children learn this at a young age, the knowledge of their own inner wisdom accompanies them through their sometimes difficult growing up years, and is with them for life.

Guidelines for Doing Imagery with Children

1. Remember that children are naturals with imagery. They generally need less preparation, and sometimes they leave their eyes open.

2. Reassure them that you will be with them while they look inside with their imaginations.

3. When first doing imagery with children, special place and a visit with a heart friend are good places to start.

4. Take some notes while your child is journeying. This will spur your memory as you later refer to this imagery.

5. If the child is experiencing panic, you can begin for them, helping to create some distance between the child and his or her panic. Ask them to see themselves in a safe place.

6. Children usually make easier transitions from inner to outer world. Have them open their eyes and make some physical contact with them when the imagery is complete.

7. Talk about their imagery with them. Find out how they feel about it.

8. Help them with integration by finding a way to remind them on a regular basis of the imagery they have done (a picture they draw about the imagery, a stuffed animal that is similar to one they have seen, etc.).

Guiding Children in Special Place / Heart Friend Imagery

1. Take some moments for yourself. Relax. Center yourself with breathing, awareness of the ground beneath you, and prayer.
2. Tell the child what you will be doing and asking, and give reassurance of your presence the whole time ("I will be right here with you").
3. Encourage the child to relax. If extra help is needed, encourage the child to be like jello or wet noodles. If extra help is still needed, ask the child to relax each body part, from toes to head, guiding this with words (ex: Let your toes relax completely, and then your ankles. Breathe and relax. Now relax your legs, etc.").
4. Say, "Imagine yourself in a place that feels safe and good. A place where you love to be."
5. Recruit the child's inner senses by asking, "What colors do you see here?"," What sounds do you notice?", "What is around you?", "Is it daytime or nighttime?", and "Where are you in this scene?".
6. Have the child focus on their heart, and call for a heart friend to come forth (tell the child this friend can be anything or anyone).
7. Guide the child through the five essential ingredients of the recipe with these questions:
    - "Greet your friend and thank your friend for coming."
    - "Ask your friend if it has a message for you...something to show or tell you."
    - "Ask your friend if it needs anything"
    - "Ask whether anything needs to happen."
    - (optional) Is there a way that you can be even better friends?
    - "Thank your friend for coming and say Good-bye."

8. Remember that you can have the child call for a helper if the imagery seems stuck.
9. Stay with the child while transitioning out of imagery into the physical world. Touch can be helpful.
10. Ask the child, "How do you feel?"
11. Find ways to help the child with integration, bringing the journey and inner images into the physical world of the child (art, objects, stories).

Guiding Children into Imagery with Health Issues

1. Take some moments for yourself. Relax. Center yourself with breathing, awareness of the ground beneath you, and prayer.
2. Tell the child what you will be doing and asking, and give reassurance.
3. Encourage the child to relax. If extra help is needed, encourage the child to be like jello or wet noodles. If extra help is still needed, ask the child to relax each body part, from toes to head, guiding this with words (ex: "let your toes relax completely, and then your ankles. Breathe and relax. Now relax your legs," etc.).
4. Say, "Imagine yourself in a place that feels safe and good. A place where you love to be."
5. Recruit the child's inner senses by asking, "What colors do you see?" "What sounds do you notice?", "What is around you?", "Is it daytime or nighttime?", and "where are you in this scene?"
6. Ask the child to invite a healing helper to come. Have the child take some time to befriend this helper. Guide the child like this: "Say hello.", "Thank this helper for coming.", "Is there something your helper wants to show or tell you?"
7. With the healing helper at the child's side, have the child look at the body part in question...at the illness or injury. Say, "Invite this part to come to you as a picture".
8. Help the child to dialogue with the image. Say, "Notice everything carefully.", "Does this part of your body have something to show or tell you?", "What does this part of you need?"
9. With the healing helper at the child's side, have the child call forth an image of health in this same area.

193

Say, "What would this same area look like if it were healthy and strong?".

10. Have the child inquire as to what needs to happen. You can have the child ask the healing helper what needs to happen. Take special note of any images of movement from the state of disease to the state of health, so you can help the child to affirm this movement in words and pictures.

11. Close the imagery by guiding the child to say good-bye, thanking all those who have come.

12. Stay with the child while transitioning out of imagery into the physical world. Touch can be helpful.

13. Ask the child, "how do you feel?"

14. Find ways to help the child with integration, bringing the journey and inner images into the physical world of the child (art, objects, and healing affirmations based on the inner pictures of health and the wisdom acquired from the child's inner world).

"All know that the drop merges into the ocean but few know that the ocean merges into the drop"

Kabir

Chapter Twenty Four
Different Imagery Styles

The formulas that are taught in this book help to provide a strong container in which deep inner imagery can take place and be received. Different names for this type of imagery include interactive imagerysm, spontaneous imagery, deep imagery, and non-directed imagery. Regardless of the name by which it is called, this is imagery that is beckoned into form and is then "seen" and "heard." For the most part, the imagery that this book examines and explores is this type of non-directed and spontaneous imagery, arising from within. In this book, I have called it deep imagery.

A whole category of imagery that has not been explored here is controlled imagery. This type of imagery offers words or suggestions to which the body/mind responds. Controlled or directed imagery is often used as a means of engagement, allowing the body and mind to relax deeply through the purposeful engagement of the senses. An example of this might be the suggestion to imagine yourself by the sea, smelling the salt air, feeling the sand beneath your feet and the sun against your skin, and hearing the sound of the waves and the cries of the gulls. This type of imagery is directed imagery and is the basis for guided relaxation.

An oft-cited example of this type of imagery uses the image of a lemon to illustrate the body-mind connection. You are asked to imagine the lemon, the color and shape of it, the texture of the skin, and the weight and feeling of it in your hand. Then you imagine opening the lemon's skin with a knife, seeing the squirting of its juice, and smelling its citrusy aroma. Is your mouth watering? A physical response is common as your salivary glands are activated by the image. The body responds to the image the mind is holding. Of course, we are all different, and the lemon you see will be slightly different from the lemon I see. But generally, most people share a common group of responses.

A clearer example of individual uniqueness in imagery can be explored with the image of a familiar object like a teacup. When asked to imagine a teacup, you may envision a particular teacup that sits in your cupboard as you read this. You may envision a teacup that belonged to your grandmother. Or, you may envision a teacup that you have never before seen. Individual differences will be unique. You are responding to an external request to envision a teacup. Your mind is following instructions. Ideas for images are given, and the individual mind selects a unique image in response to the given instruction. The mind and body respond to the suggestion. This is one way in which old images that are no longer serving us can be replaced with new, healing images. The basic difference between directed and non-directed imagery lies in the source. In directed imagery your body/mind is *responding* to external direction and suggestion. In non-directed imagery (deep imagery) you are calling forth the images from the deep pool of knowing that lies within you. *You* are calling the images forth and giving them life.

In general, working with directed imagery yields a more structured journey. The unknown is held at bay. The image is chosen by the mind (yours or someone else's), and the body and mind respond. The deeper places of the psyche are less prominent in directed imagery. Still, controlled or directed imagery can be of great value in many applications. The golfer who imagines the perfect swing in all its detail will imprint that action on his or her mind. The body will respond. The dancer who imagines his or her performance in flawless detail will be prepared on one more level to embrace the stage. This phenomenon is often called imagery rehearsal. It can be applied to nearly any situation. I like to illustrate imagery rehearsal by sharing a quote from baseball champion Babe Ruth. When asked what he thought about when he struck out, he is reported to have replied, "I think about hitting home runs!"

Directed imagery is also extremely valuable during emergency situations. The mind is given a suggestion or a task that will be helpful to the situation at hand. Calming and relaxing the mind and body, especially during crisis, can be a difficult business. Directed imagery cuts right to the quick. As a nurse, I was often called upon to help care for people with chronic lung disease. A terrible panic results from the inability to breathe. I would direct these patients with a calm voice and have them imagine plenty of air coming into their lungs as I guided them into a slower, deeper breathing pattern. I would breathe with them and ask them to remember a time when they were at peace, inviting them to allow their bodies to remember this time. These simple directions became strong medicine for them during their time of crisis. Body-mind intervention enhanced the other treatments they were receiving and helped them through a time of fear and uneasiness.

The body itself can be called upon to assume qualities that are needed or wanted because they are lacking. In this type of imagery, you remember a time when you embodied the needed quality, or you clearly bring to mind someone who embodies this quality. You "see" yourself radiating this quality, and then you bring the scene forward, seeing yourself in the here and now, full of joy, peace, or whatever quality you are seeking to receive. Your body remembers what it has held and where it has been. You can also borrow what you have seen in others, try it on, and become familiar with it. This remembering, borrowing and trying on can become a bridge to a new way of being.

I mention these forms of imagery briefly because they are valuable and available. For those of you who want to know more, I have listed a number of sources in the bibliography.

The imagery I have taught here through the template of the "recipe" is perhaps more appropriately called a receptive type of imagery-- imagery that teaches us to listen first rather than readily implementing the changes we desire. One is not bad and the other good. They are just different. With deep imagery the field is wide open for experimentation and exploration. I have experienced some wonderful imagery that involved imagining myself in a scene from the history of my spiritual tradition. I have conversed with great works of art through imagery. I have experimented with putting events between myself and Spirit and holding them in blessing in this way. I have journeyed with the great archetypes. I have journeyed with mind, body, and Spirit. Time has become elastic as I journeyed into the past and into the future. The possibilities are truly endless. When the time is perfect, I plan to have a conversation with the moon.

If we learn to listen "with the ears of our heart," (These words are from the teachings of St. Benedict. I first heard them from my teacher, E. S. Gallegos, during my first initiation into imagery), much can be learned. Our deepest selves want to see us through to our most fruitful place of being, so they offer us the images and remembrances that carry us forward to where we need to be.

Every human person is unique, and styles of learning are as unique as responses to life. Explore what is best for you. A unique style of looking within will emerge for you as you gain comfort in the world of imagery. Life will assist you as you broaden your knowledge of imagery. You will meet people, talk with them, and learn things from them. Books and articles will find their way to you. And most of all, you will learn of the inner world from the center of that world, which is within you.

Chapter Twenty Five

Infinity Meets Infinity

Communion with the Universe

The inner world is truly a new field of learning, a frontier. Endless territories within us await our exploration. Endless possibilities exist for communion and discovery. All of life, all of nature, pain, beauty, and every disparity and divergence can be touched and known in a new way when we converse with it from the depths of our being. Truly, no limits exist.

When I was a small child, I was totally amazed by the concept of infinity. My mind just could not embrace this concept! I can remember how the thought of the endlessness of the universe almost hurt my brain. Now in my adult life I return to this thought, having learned that the capacity to journey into infinity exists not only outside of us but also within us! Our inner being, in its infinite vastness, is a counterpart for the infinity of the physical universe. I am still amazed. Inside of us is a portal that denies no interchange. If I wanted to converse with infinity, I would not need to grab hold of it with my mind! I could go inside and invite an image that would represent infinity to come forth. I could talk with that image; listen to it, converse with it. In the inner world the possibilities for discourse are limitless.

If you want to talk with a flower, an heirloom, a great painting, an ancient tree, with a feeling, with an experience, you go to that place inside you where you can greet it, where you can become receptive enough to listen, look, and discover what it has to show you or tell you, where you can discern the beginning of its message to you, where the conversation can begin. Often, with a great work of art or a natural phenomenon, the conversation has actually begun as your external awareness beholds the other. The object or other has itself begun the conversation as it comes into your awareness. You perceive it with your outer senses. Something about it "stands out;" something "comes forward." Something touches you in some way. This experience is the beginning. You can learn of the world from the world itself. You allow the conversation to begin, and you can enter into it.

External resources are available in profusion in this day and age. We seek resources to assist us in the exploration of ourselves, the world in which we live, and the entirety of creation. The knowledge and discoveries of those who came before us are truly at our fingertips. This mass of human information begs us now for balance. That balance can be found by crossing through the border of our earthly bodies and entering the unexplored peripheries and territories of the inner realms. It is here, on the inside, that we as humans can truly know that we are not distinctly separate from anything or anyone. This is the root place of peace, of compassion, and of understanding.

This place inside, this core that is fed by the deep rivers of your soul, is where you know without doubt that you are connected to everything else. Having touched the ground of this inner place, you discover nothing is the same. You become a part of all that is, not because this is a new event, but because you become aware in your deepest place of understanding that you are so very not alone. You exist as a unique being in total communion with your Creator and with all creation.

Your inner world awaits you. Everything and everyone you have ever known or seen can become your teacher in this world. Your deepest self will not lead you astray, but will show you your own unique paths to healing, growing, and the realization of who you are. Your inner world will enrich your life and help you navigate life's events. You are the pioneer of this amazing frontier.

Gratitude

I wish to thank everyone who has helped along the way to make this book a reality. My thanks extend to my imagery teacher, Steve Gallegos, and to my colleagues in the field of Deep Imagery. Thanks for the learning, the guiding, and the opportunities to guide. Thanks also to The Academy for Guided Imagery and their wonderful teachers, and to beautiful Santa Sabina Retreat Center in San Rafael, CA….a place that captured my heart and kissed my soul.

To my friends and colleagues who reviewed this manuscript and offered feedback, advice, and support, I extend my heartfelt gratitude. Colleen Brenneman, Sharon Pennypacker, Jeff Gunzenhauser, Bill Montague, Lynn Keller, and Pat Morgan. Deep thanks also go to Celia Finestone, Dana Pratt, Sandy Silva, and Heather Leigh-Gary.

And to Jack Silknetter, the king of the red pen…a very special Thank You!

To my dear family, you have been part of this project in the ways of silent support, love, and understanding…Al, Lyssie, Rini, and Laddie, endless thanks to each of you!

To everyone who has graciously given me permission to have their journeys become part of this book. You have shared so generously.

Back cover photograph credit goes to Judith Giddings. Web page photo credit goes to Penny Bailey-Mase. Thank you, Judith and Penny!

And lastly, to the imagery itself…and the journeys that have emerged from myself and others, which have become part of this book and part of this teaching. Namaste'

Bibliography

Bodo, Murray , O.F.M. <u>The Way Of St. Francis</u>. New York: Doubleday, 1984.

Bodo, Murray, O.F.M. <u>Through The Year With Francis Of Assisi</u>. New York: Doubleday, 1987.

Bressler, David E., PHD, and Rossman, Martin L.,MD <u>Preparing Patients For Surgery with Interactive Guided Imagery sm.</u> Live Workshop Tapes, Los Angeles: Academy For Guided Imagery, May 7, 2000.

Bressler, David E., PHD, and Rossman, Martin L.,MD <u>Treating Depression With Interactive Guided Imagery sm</u>. Live Workshop Tapes, Los Angeles: Academy For Guided Imagery, May 7, 2000.

Campbell, Joseph. <u>A Joseph Campbell Companion</u>. Edited and selected by Diane K. Olson. New York: HarperCollins, 1991.

De Mello, Anthony. <u>Sadhana</u>. New York: Doubleday, 1984.

De Mello, Anthony. <u>Wellsprings</u>. New York: Doubleday, 1986.

Elias, Jason and Ketcham, Katherine. <u>Feminine Healing</u>. New York: Warner Books Inc., 1995.

Gallegos, Eligio Stephen, PhD., <u>Animals Of the Four Windows.</u> Santa Fe: Moon Bear Press, 1991.

Gallegos, Eligio Stephen, PhD., <u>The Personal Totem Pole</u> . Santa Fe: Moon Bear Press, 1985.

Goodwin, Gail. <u>Heart</u>. New York: HarperCollins, 2002.

Goudge, Elizabeth. <u>The Scent Of Water</u>. New York: Pyramid Books, 1963.

Hay, Louise. "Dear Louise," <u>Science Of Mind</u>. September 2003.

Judith, Anodea. <u>Wheels of Life</u>. St. Paul, MN: Llewellyn Publications, 2002.

Kidd, Sue Monk. <u>When The Heart Waits</u>. San Francisco: HarperCollins, 1992.

Lewis, C. S., <u>The Four Loves</u>. N.Y.: Harcourt, Brace, and World, Inc., 1960.

Lohr, James E. and Migdow, Jeffrey A., <u>Breathe In Breathe Out</u>. Alexandria, VA: Time Life Books, 1986.

Mengelkoch, Louise, MA, and Nerburn, Kent, PHD, ed., <u>Native American Wisdom</u>, San Rafael, CA.: New World Library, 1991.

Myss, Caroline. <u>Sacred Contracts</u>. New York: Harmony Books, 2001.

Naparstek, Belleruth. <u>Health Journeys: Successful Surgery</u>. Audio CD set. Image Paths Inc. Akron, Ohio. 1992.

Naparstek, Belleruth. Health Journeys: Total Wellness. Audio CD set. Time Warner Audiobooks, New York, 2001.

Northrup, Christiane, MD. Women's Bodies, Women's Wisdom. New York: Bantam Books, 1998.

O'Donohue, John. Beauty. New York: HarperCollins, 2004.

Pony Boy, GaWaNi. Horse, Follow Closely. Irvine, CA: Bowtie Press, 1998.

Rossman, Martin L., MD. Guided Imagery For Self-Healing. Tiburon, CA: HJ Kramer Inc., 2000.

Steiger, Brad. Totems. San Francisco: HarperCollins, 1997.

Weil, Andrew, M.D. and Rossman, Martin, M.D. Self-healing With Guided Imagery: How To Use The Power Of Your Mind To Heal Your Body. Audiocassette. Boulder, CO:Sounds True, 2004.

Whyte, David. The Heart Aroused. New York: Doubleday, 1994.

Resources

Visit my web site for inspiration, journey ideas, calendar, and contact information. I lead groups of all sizes in the exploration of deep imagery, and combine this with gentle yoga upon request.

Jenny Garrison R.N.
P.O.Box 362
Wellsboro, PA 16901
www.imageryinyou.com

The following organizations can help you to further your education and training in the use of imagery. With these resources, you can find a guide or practitioner near you, or provide yourself with further information on the use of healing imagery.

International Association for Visualization Research
P.O. box 175
Coyote, NM 87012
www.deepimagery.org.

The Academy for Guided Imagery
30765 Pacific Coast Highway #369
Malibu, CA 90265
www.academyforguidedimagery.com

Beyond Ordinary Nursing
P.O. Box 8177
Foster City, CA 94404
www.integrativeimagery.com

The Healing Mind
1341 S. Eliseo Drive
Greenbrae, CA 94904
www.thehealingmind.org

Healthjourneys
891 Moe Dr., suite C
Akron OH 44310
www.healthjourneys.com

Imagery International
1574 Coburg Rd. #555
Eugene OR 97401
www.imageryinternational.org.

Printed in the United States
79163LV00002B/292-339